AND PERSONALITY TESTS

IQ
AND PERSONALITY TESTS

Assess your creativity, aptitude and intelligence

Philip Carter

KoganPage

LONDON PHILADELPHIA NEW DELHI

Publisher's note

Every possible effort has been made to ensure that the information contained in this book is accurate at the time of going to press, and the publishers and authors cannot accept responsibility for any errors or omissions, however caused. No responsibility for loss or damage occasioned to any person acting, or refraining from action, as a result of the material in this publication can be accepted by the editor, the publisher or any of the authors.

First published in Great Britain in 2007 by Kogan Page Limited
Reprinted 2010, 2012

120 Pentonville Road	1518 Walnut Street, Suite 1100	4737/23 Ansari Road
London N1 9JN	Philadelphia PA 19102	Daryaganj
United Kingdom	USA	New Delhi 110002
www.koganpage.com		India

© Philip Carter, 2007

British Library Cataloguing in Publication Data

A CIP record for this book is available from the British Library.

ISBN   978 0 7494 6856 9

Typeset by Saxon Graphics Ltd, Derby
Printed and bound in India by Replika Press Pvt Ltd

Contents

Introduction

The British Psychological Society defines a psychometric test as 'an instrument designed to produce a quantitive assessment of some psychological attribute or attributes'.

Psychometric tests are basically tools for measuring the mind and are frequently used by employers as part of their selection process. Employers believe that such tests considerably assist them in providing an accurate assessment of whether an individual is able to do the required job and whether the person's character is suited to the work. A meaning of the word 'metric' is 'measure', and 'psycho' means 'mind'.

Psychometric tests have existed since the turn of the 19th century, although attempts to measure the differences between the psychological characteristics of individuals can be traced back to Hippocrates around 400 BC, who attempted to define four basic temperament types as optimistic, depressed, irritable and sluggish.

In the last 25–30 years, psychometric tests have been brought into widespread use in industry because of the need by employers to ensure they place the right people in the right job from the outset. One of the main reasons for this in today's competitive world of tight purse strings, cost-cutting and low budgets is the high cost of errors, including the need to readvertise and reinterview new applicants, and reinvestment in training. There can also be serious difficulties involved in dispensing with the services of someone who has just been hired, especially if a contract has been signed. Furthermore, if a new recruit causes personality conflicts within a team or department, this may lead to unrest between other members of staff with the result that the team may underperform.

Although an organization will not found its entire decision on the basis of an individual's test results, the use of psychometric testing in selection is now well-established, and can be used to provide objective information about different areas of a candidate's skills, for example the extent of their knowledge, motivations, personality and potential.

The two main types of psychometric tests used are personality questionnaires and aptitude tests. Aptitude tests are designed to assess a person's abilities, and personality questionnaires help to build up a profile of an individual's characteristics and personality. It is important that such tests are evaluated in tandem with each other as it does not necessarily mean that if a person scores well in an aptitude test that they will be suited to the job, as, whilst you may be good at doing something, you may dislike it intensely, and success in most tasks depends on your personal qualities and your attitude.

Personality refers to the patterns of thought, feeling and behaviour that are unique to every one of us, and these are the characteristics that distinguish us from other people. Our personality implies the predictability about how we are likely to act or react under different circumstances. In reality, of course, nothing is that simple and our reactions to situations are never so predictable. In many ways, the word 'personality' defies a simple definition, so broad is its usage.

Although, through the years, theorists have emphasized different aspects of personality, and have disagreed about its development and effect on behaviour, it is accepted generally that heredity and development combine and interact to form our basic personality. In addition to heredity, many psychologists believe that critical periods exist in personality development, and these periods are when we are most sensitive to a particular type of environmental event, for example when we are developing our understanding of language and how well our basic needs are met in infancy, which can leave a permanent mark on our personality. Very loosely, therefore, a **personality test** is any device or instrument for assessing or evaluating personality.

Although personality questionnaires are usually referred to as tests, this can be misleading as they do not have pass or fail scores. They are designed to measure attitudes, habits and values, and are not usually timed. Sometimes these questionnaires are incorporated into the employer's application form and sometimes they are used during the second stage procedure.

The personality tests in this book are designed to measure a range of aspects of your character and make-up in a fun, light-hearted and entertaining way. Although preparation or practice does not affect the outcome of this type of questionnaire, it is, nevertheless, helpful to familiarize yourself with typical questions and typical test structure, and it is always a useful, and often revealing exercise to use these tests to analyse yourself from time to time, and also have fun analysing your friends and family.

There is no requirement to read through these tests first before attempting them, just the need to answer them intuitively, and without too much consideration. There is no right or wrong response. Whenever you are faced with a personality question-naire, then it is necessary to answer the questions correctly. Any attempt to guess what you think is the correct answer, in other words the answer that you think your prospective employer wants to hear, is likely to be spotted when your answers are being analysed, as tests often guard against such manipulation by posing the same question more than once, but in a different way. At all times, simply follow the instructions and be honest with your answers.

Aptitude tests, or as they are perhaps better known, cognitive, ability or intelligence tests, do not examine your general knowledge, but are designed to give an objective assessment of the candidate's abilities in a number of disciplines, for example in verbal understanding, numerical, logic, and spatial, or diagrammatic reasoning skills. Unlike personality tests, aptitude tests are marked and may have a cut-off point above which you pass and below which you fail or need to be assessed again. Intelligence tests, or IQ (intelligence quotient) tests are standardized after being given to many thousands of people and an average IQ (100) established, a score above or below this norm being used, according to a bell curve, to establish the subject's actual IQ rating.

Whilst it is accepted that IQ is hereditary and remains constant throughout life, and, therefore, it is not possible to increase your actual IQ, it is possible to improve your performance in IQ tests by practising the many different types of questions, and learning to recognize the recurring themes. The aptitude tests in the second part of this book are typical of the type and style of question you are likely to encounter in actual tests and will provide valuable practice for anyone who may have to take this type of test in the future.

Employers use aptitude tests to find out if the candidate has the ability to fit the required vacancy and they can also be used to identify suitable jobs for people within an organization. These tests can be helpful to both the employer and the candidate in identifying strengths and weaknesses, and thus help to find the job for which you are most suited.

Psychometric testing is likely to become even more popular and widely used by employers in the future. In the United States, the Graduate Record Examination for graduate entry into universities is being replaced over the next few years by a Computer Adaptive Test, which is an interactive form of testing where the questions are set in relation to the ease with which questions have been answered.

The latest trend in psychometric testing is ever more towards online testing. This will enable, or even require, candidates to complete and submit their test in advance of being shortlisted, thus enabling the employer to have the results in advance of the interview. Candidates will have ample opportunity to practise on similar tests in the coming months and years as sample tests proliferate on the internet.

Personality Tests

How to do the personality tests

This section of the book consists of 20 tests designed to assess different aspects of your personality, including your laterality, creative and perceptual skills. There are three different types of questionnaires in the first 18 of these tests, as shown below. In each of these, you are presented with a statement or question relating to some aspect of your personality and are asked to respond to it in one of several ways according to the instructions given at the start of each test:

1. Respond on a scale of 1–5, with 5 being the most applicable to yourself, down to 1 being most untrue.
2. Answer a question or statement by choosing which one of the three alternative responses given is most applicable to you.
3. Rank four statements in a group according to which is most true to your character, down to which is most unlike your character.

The procedure for completing each of these is to answer the questions as truthfully and realistically as possible; in other words, be true to yourself at all times in order to obtain the most accurate assessment. There are no right or wrong answers and there is no time limit for completing the tests.

How well do you cope under pressure?

1. How important to you is the need to succeed?

    a. Quite important
    b. Very important
    c. It is not something I think about a great deal

2. How often have you taken time off work due to stress?

    a. Twice or less
    b. More than twice
    c. Never

3. Do you believe you are a person who is thought of by others as someone who is able to keep a cool head in a crisis?

    a. Sometimes, but often someone who keeps a cool head in a crisis does not have a grasp of the situation
    b. Not really
    c. Yes, that is how I believe others rightly perceive me

4. Which of the following would you say would be most beneficial to reducing stress and enabling you to relax after a particularly busy day at the office?

   a. A couple of hours' sleep in my favourite armchair
   b. A nice stiff whisky or other spirit
   c. Eat a bar of chocolate

5. Does working to deadlines give you a buzz?

   a. No, but working to deadlines is a necessary evil most of us have to cope with
   b. No, I find working to deadlines quite a worry and much prefer being able to set my own pace
   c. Yes, I believe I work well under pressure

6. Do you believe that modern living creates much more pressure than say, 40 years ago?

   a. Perhaps
   b. Yes
   c. No

7. You are suddenly asked to look after your nephew's three unruly children for the weekend due to a family crisis. How would you feel about doing this?

   a. It would worry me
   b. I would find the thought of it so horrendous that I would probably try to get out of doing it
   c. I would relish the challenge

8. Have you ever damaged anything due to feeling the pressure?

   a. Not actually damaged anything although I have done such things as slamming down the phone on occasions
   b. Yes
   c. No

9. Do you find that little, almost insignificant things, occasionally upset you?

   a. Yes, occasionally
   b. More than occasionally
   c. Rarely or never

10. What do you feel about having to get to grips with new technology?

   a. Quite indifferent about it. If I have to get to grips with it because of my job, for example, then it is usually something I am able to cope with
   b. It worries me somewhat
   c. It is something I enjoy and find of interest

11. What do you think, for you, is the main purpose of weekends?

   a. A time when I can spend more time with my friends and family
   b. A time when I don't have to work quite as hard as I do the rest of the week. However, I am not in a position where I can completely switch off
   c. A time for giving myself a mental and emotional break

12. When your house is being decorated, or when you are having other alterations carried out, how do you feel?

   a. It does not bother me in particular as these things have to be done
   b. Somewhat on edge until it is completed, especially as it disturbs my routine
   c. Quite happy about it and sometimes quite excited depending upon what is being done

13. Do you have friends whom you trust completely and can talk to in turbulent times?

    a. Maybe
    b. Not really
    c. Yes

14. Do you feel that more than ever we are living today in a competitive world?

    a. I would say that the modern world is perhaps a little more competitive than a generation or so ago
    b. Yes, very much so
    c. No more competitive than it was

15. Do you ever discuss your feelings with other people?

    a. Occasionally
    b. Rarely or never
    c. More than occasionally

16. Do you believe in pushing yourself harder and harder?

    a. Sometimes
    b. Yes, that is the best way to make a success out of life
    c. No, life's too short

17. How do you feel about having several tasks on the go at the same time?

    a. It does not bother me
    b. I prefer one job at a time
    c. I prefer having several tasks on the go at the same time

18. How often do you get angry and upset with yourself if you make a mistake or things do not go the way you expected?

    a.   Occasionally, as I suppose do most people

    b.   Probably more than the average person

    c.   Probably less than the average person

19. Have you ever taken any sort of medication, including pills, in order to relieve stress?

    a.   Occasionally

    b.   More than occasionally

    c.   Never

20. Has your own health ever suffered due to the death or illness of a loved one?

    a.   No, but maybe it would do in the future, I just do not know

    b.   Yes

    c.   No, I have coped with, and have suffered, grief and upset, as have all of us, but my own health has never suffered as a result

21. Have you ever suffered from stress due to the pressure of taking examinations?

    a.   Perhaps I find taking examinations a little stressful but no more than the average person

    b.   Yes

    c.   No

22. What are your views on alternative therapy such as acupuncture in order to relieve stress?

    a.   Not sure, perhaps it is something I might consider if the need arose

    b.   It is not something I would consider

    c.   It can be very beneficial

23. Do you ever get stressed out by the thought of doing small household chores such as washing up or cutting the lawn?

    a. Not stressed, although such tasks can sometimes be something of an annoyance
    b. Yes
    c. Never

24. How easy is it for you to switch off completely, put everything completely out of your mind and totally relax?

    a. Sometimes it is more difficult to switch off than at other times
    b. It is almost, if not, impossible
    c. I am in the fortunate position of finding it reasonably easy to switch off completely

25. How often have you felt the pressure of one thing and another is simply doing your head in?

    a. Occasionally
    b. More often than I would like
    c. Rarely or never

26. You are sitting in a traffic jam. Which of the following is likely to be your strongest feeling?

    a. Anger
    b. Frustration
    c. Boredom

27. Do you feel more, or less, pressure the older you get?

    a. About the same
    b. More
    c. Less

28. What would be your feelings on moving to another house?

    a.   Well, I quite like the house we live in now but perhaps a
         move at this time could have its advantages
    b.   An overwhelming task to be avoided if at all possible
    c.   A lot of hard work, but generally something to plan for,
         and look forward to

29. How often has your sex life ever suffered due to stress or
    pressure of work?

    a.   On no more than a couple of occasions
    b.   More than a couple of occasions
    c.   Never

30. Have you ever suffered from stress due to having to give up
    something such as caffeine or nicotine?

    a.   Not apart from a few withdrawal symptoms
    b.   Yes
    c.   No

Analysis

All of us experience different degrees of pressure and stress at
some time in our lives but we deal with it in different ways. Some
causes of stress are perhaps easier to deal with than others. The
taking of school examinations, for example, is a common cause
of stress. However, because we know for a number of years in
advance that these exams will take place we have time to prepare
ourselves both mentally and by taking mock examinations and by
revising.

    The real examinations of life are, however, not so predictable.
The following is a list of some common events and experiences
that can cause stress; it is when these events occur unexpectedly

and simultaneously (the double or triple whammy) that we are at our most vulnerable:

- death of a partner;
- divorce/separation/break up of a relationship;
- death of a close relative or friend;
- personal illness;
- illness of a loved one;
- moving house;
- redundancy;
- large mortgage/debts;
- children leaving home;
- changes at work – new job, boss, responsibilities.

Common responses to stress include loss of sleep, irritability, short temper, worry and stress-related ailments. Dealing with responses to stress can be difficult, as what one person finds stressful or pressurizing, another may not, and we all react to different stressful situations in different ways. Nevertheless, a good starting point is increasing your awareness of the main causes of pressure and stress, as this, at the very least, could help you in trying to see what you can do about it.

You can take several suggested steps to combat stress or the effects of pressure:

1. Sometimes, the best cure is prevention and an analysis of the type of situations that you have found pressurizing in the past should enable you to look out for similar situations that may occur in the future, and enable you to recognize any warning signs that you are about to enter into a similarly stressful period.
2. It is, of course, desirable to take some sort of exercise to keep yourself in good shape, especially in times of stress.
3. It is also desirable to try to get a good night's sleep and, if possible, especially when sleep is proving impossible, due to

the number of negative thoughts racing through your head, confront the cause of the pressure by writing down the thoughts that are occurring to you and then attempt to analyse and evaluate them.

4. It is also necessary to talk to people about the pressures that you are experiencing. In other words, do not bottle things up inside you. Confide in a friend, partner or relative, even, if necessary, a professional counsellor. It may be that after talking things through in this way, your fears may be put into perspective and the pressures no longer feel so great.

5. When the pressure is work-related it is necessary to discipline yourself to switch off from the situation that is causing the pressure. This may be achieved by reserving weekends for yourself and your family in order to give yourself an emotional and mental break. If this is not possible, then try to organize a longer break. If this does not seem possible due to the pressures and workload that have built up, remember that no one is indispensable and that the most important thing is your health and mental well-being.

Assessment

Award yourself 2 points for every 'c' answer, 1 point for every 'a' and 0 points for every 'b'.

45–60 points

Your score indicates that you cope with pressure extremely well. You are likely to be thought of by others as someone who is extremely laid-back and almost totally relaxed, and you are able to keep things in proportion at almost all times. The only word of caution about being in the fortunate position of having this temperament and attitude is that you should still be prepared for potentially pressurizing situations that will inevitably occur. You should, in other words, have the ability to plan for pressures and build in leeway for the unexpected. It is also worth remembering that a certain amount of tension is positive as people do respond to, and are encouraged by, challenges.

31–44 points

Whilst you do find yourself pressurized and stressed out on occasions, this tends to be the exception rather than the rule and, more importantly, such situations are never long-lasting. As a result you are able to switch off somewhat where necessary and not push yourself too far. You appear to be in the fortunate position of being able to look after yourself when you are facing pressure and you have the ability to say no if someone is making unreasonable demands.

Less than 30 points

Your score indicates that you are affected by pressure in a negative way. As society's code of conduct prevents many of the natural releases of pent-up emotions such as by violent means or by running away from the situation, pressure can, therefore, build up inside you and this is when you are at your most vulnerable to stress. It is at these times that you may have a tendency to build things up out of all proportion. However, it is worth remembering that most of the things that we worry about never happen, that most of the pressures that build up are short-term events and that if we deal with these pressures in a measured and structured way we should not be affected by them quite so badly. After all, these types of pressures are not restricted to just ourselves; they are the same pressures that are felt, at some time, by all people throughout the world.

You should also be conscious of the fact that pressure does lead to stress and many illnesses are stress-related. It is, therefore, essential that in pressurized situations you try to take one step back and reflect on your current situation, and your life in general and the positive things – there will be many – that exist and are occurring.

In general, try to develop a more positive attitude when dealing with what are termed modern-day pressures, but in fact are the same pressures that have always existed in some form for past generations. In fact, modern research should enable us to cope with these pressures better than we ever did in the past. At least now we recognize the danger of such situations.

Such a positive approach may include analysing and recognizing the cause or causes of the pressure, your reactions to this pressure and your ways of coping with the pressure. It may also include changing your way of thinking about the pressure, improving the way you do things, for example in a work situation, and knowing the best source of help and the right people to talk to when necessary.

It is also essential that you look after yourself when facing pressure, not just for your own well-being but also for the benefit of those closest to you. This can be achieved in several ways, for example:

- As well as doing the things that are absolutely necessary, do the fun things that you and those close to you most enjoy.
- Try not to be too self-critical as we all make mistakes.
- Give yourself a break.
- Try to relax and sleep more.
- Keep yourself fit.
- Eat and drink sensibly.
- Cultivate other interests.

Are you a people person?

In each of the following, choose from a scale of 1–5 which of these statements you most agree with or is most applicable to you. Choose just one of the numbers 1–5 in each of the 36 statements. Choose 5 for most agree/most applicable, down to 1 for least agree/least applicable.

1. To get the best out of people you need to drive rather than support them

    5 4 3 2 1

2. I am not a very good listener

    5 4 3 2 1

3. I would prefer to go for a long walk on my own rather than in an organized group

    5 4 3 2 1

4. I do not have a great deal of patience when listening to other people's problems

    5 4 3 2 1

5. Winning is better than enjoying

    5   4   3   2   1

6. I do not suffer fools gladly

    5   4   3   2   1

7. I am much more comfortable talking to people on a one-to-
    one basis rather than in a group discussion

    5   4   3   2   1

8. I would describe myself as more determined than cheerful

    5   4   3   2   1

9. I am a great believer that people should stand on their own
    two feet

    5   4   3   2   1

10. I do not believe in giving money to beggars on the street

    5   4   3   2   1

11. There are things more important to me than success in my
    personal relationships

    5   4   3   2   1

12. I prefer to work alone rather than as part of a team

    5   4   3   2   1

13. I am more dominant than sociable

    5   4   3   2   1

14. I like to think of myself as something of a perfectionist

    5   4   3   2   1

15. I would describe myself as someone who keeps themselves to themselves rather than someone who goes out of their way to get to know people

    5   4   3   2   1

16. I prefer to plan my own holiday than go on a pre-arranged group holiday with a set itinerary

    5   4   3   2   1

17. I dislike social gatherings

    5   4   3   2   1

18. I prefer individual sports rather than team sports

    5   4   3   2   1

19. I need to be in control rather than go with the flow

    5   4   3   2   1

20. I prefer to celebrate my birthday quietly and would not be very happy if someone threw a surprise party for me

    5   4   3   2   1

21. I do not believe I would make a very good personnel officer

    5   4   3   2   1

22. I rarely or never take part in charity fund-raising events

    5   4   3   2   1

23. It does not worry me unduly that when I speak my mind it may upset people

   5   4   3   2   1

24. I can often be intolerant of other people's views

   5   4   3   2   1

25. I do not make friends easily

   5   4   3   2   1

26. I do not look forward to big social gatherings such as weddings

   5   4   3   2   1

27. I do not usually engage in conversations with strangers sitting next to me on long journeys

   5   4   3   2   1

28. People tend to view me as more of a loner than a mixer

   5   4   3   2   1

29. I do not often seek advice from other people

   5   4   3   2   1

30. I do not consider it important to put myself in the other person's shoes in order to see their point of view

   5   4   3   2   1

31. I am more tough than tolerant

   5   4   3   2   1

32. I do not generally feel sorry for the underdog

    5   4   3   2   1

33. If a work colleague won a million pounds on the lottery I would feel more envious than pleased for them

    5   4   3   2   1

34. I am not interested in sitting on committees

    5   4   3   2   1

35. It is important to get to know the right people

    5   4   3   2   1

36. If someone telephoned me out of the blue asking me to sell raffle tickets for a charity I would probably decline

    5   4   3   2   1

Assessment

Total score 130–180

Some people have a natural interest in all other people. They are, in effect, people persons, or people watchers. They take a keen interest in everyone about them, are curious to find out more about them and anxious to interact with them. Your score indicates that you are most certainly *not* one of those people.

You are what is sometimes, perhaps unkindly, referred to as a loner, or someone who likes to keep themselves to themselves, or stands somewhat aloof from others. Whilst you do enjoy the company of others, this is usually restricted to a very close and exclusively small circle of family and friends.

This is fine as long as it is what makes you happy and provides what you like out of life and does not frustrate your ambitions. It is, however, worth remembering that no one can be an island entirely. We all depend to a certain extent on other people to make both our personal and business lives happy and successful. The more we interact with people both on a one-to-one and group basis, the more happy and successful all aspects of our lives will be. This does not necessarily have to involve going to all kinds of social gatherings and being the life and soul of the party. What it does involve is having empathy with others, having regard for their feelings and making an effort to get to know all others, irrespective of their class or status, and gaining their respect.

Keywords: disinterested, unsociable, withdrawn, diffident

Total score 91–129

Preoccupation with other people may not, to you, be one of life's most important priorities. Nevertheless, you do tend to go somewhat out of your way to be fair to all people, and treat all people in an equal manner, and you recognize that basically all people are decent and that there is no reason not to get to know them better and behave in a polite and pleasant manner towards them.

As a result of this attitude you do tend to be liked and respected by others for what you are. You prefer to treat others as you would wish them to treat you. A neighbour, for example, is someone with whom you like to exchange pleasantries, keep on the right side of, and be there for in the event of an emergency. However, you would not go out of your way to find out their life history.

Keywords: tolerant, habitual, unbiased

Total score less than 90

You are most certainly a people person. You like observing people, assessing their personalities, finding out more about them and widening your circle of friends as much as possible. In all aspects of your life you depend on other people to a great extent. In fact, without other people your life would seem empty even to the extent of making you depressed and miserable. You enjoy social gatherings immensely and find it easy to circulate at such events, making small talk effortlessly when the occasion demands it.

The plus side of this is that you recognize the importance of the involvement of others in your life. You are, in effect, a good team player and appreciate the need to have the right people on your side if your life is going to be a successful one. Your score also indicates a great deal of warmth of character, and someone who has a great deal of empathy with others, and this earns you the respect and trust of very many people. The minus side is that some people may see you as being somewhat over-inquisitive, even intrusive. However, this is more likely to be the exception rather than the rule.

Keywords: empathetic, warm-hearted, concerned, regardful

4

Asking for what you want

In each of the following, rank the four statements in each group according to which is most applicable to you, which is least applicable, and which of the remaining two are next most applicable and next least applicable.

1.

a. I try to convey the right sort of body language whenever I ask for something
b. When I ask I need to be clear about my requirements and stick to my guns
c. If you wait until the time is right before asking you could be waiting forever
d. I think it is important to wait until the time is right before asking

2.

a. Whenever I ask for something I plan my strategy carefully in advance
b. I am a great believer in the adage 'Ask and ye shall receive'

c.   I never seem to be able to pluck up the courage to ask for what I want
d.   Whenever I ask for something I find that emphasis on humour is much more effective than boastfulness

3.

a.   I always give my potential date an escape route when asking them out, in order not to embarrass them
b.   I never seem to be able to ask anyone out for a date because I simply can never pluck up the courage
c.   I never seem to be able to ask people out on a date because of the fear of personal rejection
d.   When asking someone out for a date it is important to find out their likes and dislikes in advance

4.

a.   Whenever asking for something face to face it is important to maintain eye contact
b.   When asking for something or complaining I always try to keep a smile on my face
c.   Whenever I complain about something I fold my arms across my chest as this shows I mean business
d.   Whenever I ask for something I try to remain unemotional at all times

5.

a.   When really dissatisfied with the quality of a meal and the service in a restaurant it is a good approach to say nothing at the time, but to write a polite letter of complaint to the restaurant manager afterwards
b.   The best approach when served with a meal in a restaurant that is not up to standard is to complain immediately to the chief cook direct

c.   If I get a meal in a restaurant that is not up to standard I usually end up eating it or leaving it rather than complaining and risking making a fuss

d.   If I am not satisfied with a restaurant meal I usually point this out to the waiter and ask if he or she can take this up with the kitchen staff in order to rectify the problem

6.

a.   Whenever I ask for something I try to keep my request as specific and straightforward as possible

b.   When asking for anything, 'please' and 'excuse me' are very effective words

c.   It is important to ask with authority

d.   Empathy and sensitivity are very important when, for example, asking a friend to repay an overdue loan

Analysis

There is an old adage that states: 'You do not get anywhere in this world without asking' and another phrase that refers to some people as 'not being backward at coming forward'. It is important, however, not only to know the best way of asking for something, but also to know when is the best time to ask. Life is much more complicated than the simple philosophy of 'Ask and ye shall receive'.

One of the most important things to consider when making a request is whether the time is right. For example, it is a bad time to ask a favour from your boss first thing on a Monday morning, or when he or she has come back from a couple of days' holiday and his or her desk is submerged in paperwork.

Having decided that the time is right, then phrasing of the request is all-important. A light-hearted, even humorous remark in the first instance is helpful in creating the right atmosphere when, for example, asking for a pay rise, as long as this is then backed up by valid reasons why you believe the rise should be granted. In effect, a request for a pay rise is entering into a negotiating process, and this is why preparation is so important before making any such request.

Having decided on your approach and requirements it is essential to adopt the right attitude. It is important that you appear confident, but not cocky; relaxed and not tense; pleasant rather than confrontational; and businesslike but not emotional. It is also necessary to avoid antagonizing the person you are approaching, and this adds power to your elbow when making a complaint. You can still convey your request to the person without resorting to belligerence or being falsely apologetic. It is far better to state the complaint clearly and in a businesslike manner, and then go on to say what you think should be done about it.

At all times when making a request, ensure that you are conveying the right body language. The folding of arms conveys the wrong sort of body language and can be seen as antagonistic, as does the pointing or wagging of fingers. Equally bad is over-smiling all the time, which can be seen as condescending. Far better just to maintain eye contact, which gives an air of confidence, but not over-confidence.

Assessment

Scoring instructions (place a tick in the appropriate column for each letter):

Group	Most	Next most	Next least	Least	Score
1.					
a.	☐	☐	☐	☐	☐
b.	☐	☐	☐	☐	☐
c.	☐	☐	☐	☐	☐
d.	☐	☐	☐	☐	☐

Group	Most	Next most	Next least	Least	Score
2.					
a.	☐	☐	☐	☐	☐
b.	☐	☐	☐	☐	☐
c.	☐	☐	☐	☐	☐
d.	☐	☐	☐	☐	☐
3.					
a.	☐	☐	☐	☐	☐
b.	☐	☐	☐	☐	☐
c.	☐	☐	☐	☐	☐
d.	☐	☐	☐	☐	☐
4.					
a.	☐	☐	☐	☐	☐
b.	☐	☐	☐	☐	☐
c.	☐	☐	☐	☐	☐
d.	☐	☐	☐	☐	☐
5.					
a.	☐	☐	☐	☐	☐
b.	☐	☐	☐	☐	☐
c.	☐	☐	☐	☐	☐
d.	☐	☐	☐	☐	☐
6.					
a.	☐	☐	☐	☐	☐
b.	☐	☐	☐	☐	☐
c.	☐	☐	☐	☐	☐
d.	☐	☐	☐	☐	☐

Score 2 points for every 'a' answer ticked in Most, 3 points for every 'a' answer ticked in Next most, 1 point for every 'a' answer ticked in Next least and 0 points for every 'a' answer ticked in Least.

Score 0 points for every 'b' answer ticked in Most, 1 point for every 'b' answer ticked in Next most, 3 points for every 'b' answer ticked in Next least and 2 points for every 'b' answer ticked in Least.

Score 0 points for every 'c' answer ticked in Most, 1 point for every 'c' answer ticked in Next most, 2 points for every 'c' answer ticked in Next least and 3 points for every 'c' answer ticked in Least.

Score 3 points for every 'd' answer ticked in Most, 2 points for every 'd' answer ticked in Next most, 1 point for every 'd' answer ticked in Next least and 0 points for every 'd' answer ticked in Least.

48–72 points

Your score indicates that you have the knack of knowing just how to ask for something and on the vast majority of occasions you are successful in your request.

24–47 points

Whilst not scoring in the top range you still have the ability to ask the right question at the right time and on many occasions achieve the result you hoped for. You do, however, need to hone your skills even further and in this respect several of the suggestions made in the above analysis should prove useful.

23 points or less

Unfortunately you need to work very hard on the skills necessary in asking what, for you, are decidedly awkward questions. In fact, it may be that on many occasions you have not been successful in getting what you wanted because you were afraid to even pluck up the courage to ask in the first place.

It is true, however, that on many occasions it is necessary to ask for what you want, whether it is to ask someone out on a date, ask your boss for a pay rise, complain about bad service in a restaurant, ask a tradesperson to return and put something right that they have not done properly or ask a friend a favour. Such requests can usually only be successful if adequate thought is given to them. Sometimes it is a useful exercise to put yourself in the position of the person to whom you are making the request. For instance, how would you, in that position, best like to be approached and what attitude would you like the person making the request to adopt?

Keywords to bear in mind: planning, timing, phrasing, attitude, body language

Do you have the secret of success?

In each of the following, choose from a scale of 1–5 which of these statements you most agree with or is most applicable to you. Choose just one of the numbers 1–5 in each of the 35 statements. Choose 5 for most agree/most applicable, down to 1 for least agree/least applicable.

1. I am more of a doer than a thinker

   5   4   3   2   1

2. I am motivated more by my own inner beliefs and aspirations than the rewards it may bring

   5   4   3   2   1

3. In life you generally make your own luck, be it good or bad

   5   4   3   2   1

4. It is always too soon to quit

   5   4   3   2   1

5. I am a person who always puts in a great deal of hard work

    5   4   3   2   1

6. I am an extremely confident person

    5   4   3   2   1

7. I never abandon good intentions

    5   4   3   2   1

8. I can be ruthless when it comes to getting what I want

    5   4   3   2   1

9. I make people feel that being in my company is a rewarding
    experience, whatever their status in life

    5   4   3   2   1

10. Perfection is an impossible ideal

    5   4   3   2   1

11. It is important to give everything I do my best shot

    5   4   3   2   1

12. Success in life is much more than achieving your set goals

    5   4   3   2   1

13. I would be prepared to give up my favourite hobby, even
    though I love it dearly, if it meant success in my chosen career

    5   4   3   2   1

14. I am a very inquiring person

    5   4   3   2   1

15. I believe in grasping every opportunity that presents itself, even to the extent of taking chances

5   4   3   2   1

16. I find it easy to focus my mind on one subject for very long periods

5   4   3   2   1

17. I always look to the future

5   4   3   2   1

18. I am not a Jack of all trades, master of none person

5   4   3   2   1

19. I have no problem expressing my thoughts and feelings to others

5   4   3   2   1

20. Every day I feel I get mentally stronger

5   4   3   2   1

21. There is no such thing as a good loser, although some do show it more than others

5   4   3   2   1

22. I am not afraid of success, even though it may bring me enemies

5   4   3   2   1

23. Never give in

5   4   3   2   1

24. You do not become a success without the involvement of others

    5   4   3   2   1

25. When I am in the company of others I feel important and special

    5   4   3   2   1

26. It is possible for everyone to overcome social barriers

    5   4   3   2   1

27. I strongly believe that you must finish what you start

    5   4   3   2   1

28. I do not like to hear people boasting about their achievements

    5   4   3   2   1

29. I have far less worries than the average person

    5   4   3   2   1

30. I never do things by half-measures

    5   4   3   2   1

31. I am not nervous about making speeches to large audiences

    5   4   3   2   1

32. I am not afraid of failure

    5   4   3   2   1

33. Hard work is a means to an end

    5   4   3   2   1

34. I am clear as to where I see myself in five years' time

    5   4   3   2   1

35. I am a try, try and try again sort of person

    5   4   3   2   1

Assessment

Total score 126–175

It is sometimes said that the real secret of success is that there is no secret to success. It is certainly true that there is not just one secret of success; there are very many different factors which, when combined together, result in different levels of success for different individuals.

Your score indicates that if you are not already a success then there should be very little doubt that you will be one day, and if you are already a success then you will eventually reach even greater heights. You appear to have all the qualities necessary such as character, persistence, flair and imagination, and not least the ambition to push yourself to the heights you know you are capable of achieving.

One word of caution is that you should take care not to become a total workaholic at the expense of yourself and your family, and ultimately your happiness. If you are able to succeed in striking the right balance then you should be capable of reaching most of the goals you have set out to achieve in both your personal and working life.

Total score 90–125

You do aspire to success and have many of the necessary qualities to achieve this, but perhaps you need to work a little harder at instilling some self-confidence into yourself to make you believe you can, and will, succeed. Perhaps success is something that you dream about but never really believe will happen. It is up to you to translate these dreams into reality and remove those self-doubts. You are a hard worker, but is this hard work done in the service of others and not for you? If so, try to develop the belief that hard work brings its rewards and that some of these rewards could and should be heading in your direction. Having convinced yourself, then it may be necessary to convince others. This may not be quite so easy as it sounds, but it is certainly possible, as many have proved.

It is also useful to consider setting yourself goals. Many successful people set themselves goals that take them from where they are now to where they want to be. Such goals can be anything you want or need but when setting these goals it is also necessary to consider alternative goals, other people and other aspects of your life.

The advantage of forward planning is that you will then be clear in your mind what you really want. Having set the goals then you need to take appropriate action towards achieving these goals, you need to monitor the results you are achieving and you need to be sufficiently flexible to change, if necessary, what you are doing to achieve your goals.

Total score less than 90

A great deal of hard work and commitment is required if you are going to make a success in a chosen career. But is this what you really want out of life? You may believe that happiness is more important in life than success. In fact, for many people, happiness is success, and while happiness for many people is being a high-flyer, for others it is a stable family life, a steady job with not too much pressure and responsibility and a regular income.

Also, remember that there are different degrees of success. For many, success is holding down a regular and steady job for many years and doing that job well. For others it is reaching the top of their chosen profession, and for others, success is nothing less than fame and fortune.

6

How content are you?

1. Do you ever vent your own frustrations on other people?
   a. Occasionally
   b. Rarely or never
   c. More than occasionally

2. How often do you wish you were someone else?
   a. Not often, but occasionally I have thought that some people are luckier than me to be who they are
   b. It is something I have never seriously wished on myself
   c. I have more than occasionally wished that I was someone else

3. Do you feel that you were born under a lucky star?
   a. Perhaps I have had slightly more than my share of luck in life
   b. Most definitely
   c. No way

4. Do you ever feel you are stuck in a rut?
   a. Yes, from time to time
   b. Rarely or never
   c. Yes, I often feel frustrated that I am stuck in a rut

5. Do you feel that opportunities keep passing you by?

    a. Sometimes
    b. Rarely or never
    c. Regularly

6. If you could swap your lifestyle for a year, would you?

    a. Maybe in certain circumstances
    b. I don't believe I ever would
    c. Yes, I would relish the opportunity

7. Do you envy the rich and famous?

    a. Occasionally
    b. Rarely or never
    c. More than occasionally

8. Do you enjoy your job?

    a. Mostly, but not always
    b. Yes
    c. Generally no

9. Do you often long for exotic holidays just to get away from it all?

    a. Yes, occasionally
    b. Holidays might be nice, but they are not a necessity in my life
    c. Yes, often

10. Would you ever consider plastic surgery to improve your appearance?

    a. Perhaps
    b. No
    c. Yes

11. Do you feel that you make the most of your leisure time?

    a.   Perhaps I do not have as many leisure activities as I would like

    b.   Yes

    c.   No, because I do not have time for leisure activities

12. Do you usually get a good night's sleep?

    a.   I try to, but do not always succeed

    b.   Yes

    c.   Not usually

13. Are you envious of other people's possessions?

    a.   Occasionally

    b.   Rarely or never

    c.   More than occasionally

14. Do things ever weigh on your conscience?

    a.   Yes, perhaps sometimes they do

    b.   Rarely or never

    c.   Yes, I am a worrier in that respect

15. How do you see the future?

    a.   With a certain degree of apprehension

    b.   Hopefully things will carry on as they are now

    c.   I hope that the future will be much better than the past and present

16. Do you ever feel you have an inferiority complex?

    a.   Maybe, on occasions

    b.   No

    c.   Yes

17. Which of the following words do you think best sums you up?

    a. balanced
    b. satisfied
    c. restless

18. Have you realized most of your ambitions so far in life?

    a. Most of them
    b. I cannot think of any particular ambitions at the moment that need to be fulfilled
    c. Not at all

19. Do you feel that you have a loving and stable family life?

    a. Yes, on balance
    b. Without a doubt
    c. Not really

20. Do you have a light-hearted approach to life?

    a. Yes, with most things. However, some things are too serious to be taken light-heartedly
    b. I do try to adopt a light-hearted approach to life in general
    c. I would not describe myself as a light-hearted person

21. Are you getting the most out of life?

    a. Hopefully
    b. I believe that I am
    c. I do not believe that I am

22. How easy is it for you to sit back and relax?

    a. Sometimes it is more difficult than at other times
    b. Easy
    c. Not at all easy

23. How often do you feel frustrated about wanting to do more?
    a.   Sometimes
    b.   Rarely or never
    c.   Almost all the time

24. If you were to step back and take stock of your life, which of the following would be most applicable?
    a.   Reasonably satisfied but still feel that I could achieve much more
    b.   I would count my blessings that I have had more ups than downs in my life
    c.   I would feel somewhat angry with myself that I have not made more of my life

25. Do you often feel pleased with yourself?
    a.   Occasionally
    b.   More than occasionally
    c.   Rarely or never

Assessment

Award yourself 2 points for every 'b' answer, 1 point for every 'a' and 0 points for every 'c'.

40–50 points

One definition of being content is satisfaction with the way things are. Your score indicates that you are content with your life and therefore you are likely to have happiness and inner peace. It is this happiness that rubs off on those around you, especially your immediate family.

Even if contentment in some people means that they lack the ambition and drive of others, this is no reason to change their relaxed attitude. If they are content, then there is no reason to change, as increased success does not necessarily bring with it increased happiness. Remember the story of the man who was only happy when he was fishing. Fishing was all he ever thought about; he went fishing morning, noon and night and, as a result, he was always happy. You are in the fortunate position of having found your own niche in life. You are happy and content with your lot, and that must be the envy of many people.

25–39 points

You are satisfied with your life, although perhaps you may not realize it as much as you ought to. Although you do not lack ambition, you would never wish to pursue these ambitions at the risk of jeopardizing not just your own happiness and settled lifestyle, but of those nearest and dearest to you. There is, however, often a feeling at the back of your mind that you could achieve more, and at times you find this a little frustrating.

Despite this you do find that in general your aspirations have been fulfilled and there is, therefore, no real reason for change even if a host of other people such as friends, parents, teachers and co-workers are eager to tell you what you should do with your life. It is, after all, your life, and these goals only matter when they matter to you, and you are, therefore, the foremost expert in defining which path your own life should take.

Less than 25 points

Your score does indicate that you are in the main somewhat discontented with your life. Perhaps you feel exasperated that you have not fulfilled your ambitions or yet realized your full potential. Maybe you think that life is all too short and that you have insufficient time to do all the things you always wanted to do. Perhaps you have a job that you really do not enjoy, and while you are at your place of work you are thinking of all the other things you could be doing that really interest and stimulate you, or perhaps you are just going through one of those difficult and stressful periods in your life that all of us, from time to time, experience.

If this is the case, then now might be a good time to step back and take stock of your life, and look especially at all the positive aspects. Ask yourself what you have achieved. Maybe you have a steady job and a stable family life – in themselves no mean achievement. Perhaps you have a sport or hobby that you enjoy, and could devote more time to. Any one of these is something to be thankful for, rather than a cause for despondency.

All in all, there are many things in our lives for which we can be thankful, and there is always someone worse off than ourselves. If you are able to focus on these positives, no matter how trivial or insignificant they may seem, then there is every chance that you will begin to find the inner peace and satisfaction that seems to have so eluded you in the past.

Although we should always try to plan for the future, we can only truly be happy right now. If you do enjoy the present and make the most of what you have now, then there is every chance that this will create in itself a much better future.

7

Are you a control freak?

1. When shopping for yourself, do you prefer to shop alone or with your partner?

    a. I prefer to be with my partner
    b. No preference really
    c. I prefer to shop alone when I am buying things for myself

2. Have you ever owned or wanted to own a dog?

    a. No
    b. Yes
    c. Yes, I have a dog at present, and have had other dogs in the past

3. Do you believe the country would be a better place if you were in charge?

    a. No
    b. Maybe
    c. Yes

4. The thought of which of the following would horrify you the most?

    a.   To be on an uninhabited desert island for five years

    b.   To spend five years in prison

    c.   To be a private in the army for five years' compulsory national service

5. Do you prefer to be in charge of the television remote control?

    a.   No

    b.   Not really, it is usually just left lying around for anyone to use

    c.   Yes

6. You have just met someone in your former place of work, which you left 12 months ago. Which of the following responses would most please you when you asked them how things were at the old place?

    a.   Things are fine, everyone is very well

    b.   Much the same, things do not get any better

    c.   Things have never been as good since you left

7. Your usually submissive sex partner suddenly suggests that they take the lead in a bondage game. How would you react to this?

    a.   I would be very turned on by the suggestion

    b.   A little surprised, but would play along

    c.   Quite taken aback and somewhat uneasy about the situation

8. You find that people suddenly start referring to you by your initials, for example PJ instead of Philip. How do you feel about this?

   a. I can live with the situation, but would prefer them to use my correct name
   b. Don't mind in the slightest
   c. Rather pleased and flattered that perhaps my real name is surplus to requirements and recognition

9. Which of the following most closely resembles your own handwriting?

   a.

   b.

   c.

10. You and your partner, who are both able to drive, go out together in the same car. Who would you prefer to be driving?

    a. My partner
    b. Don't mind as we are both equally good drivers
    c. Me

11. Do you always let people finish what they are saying, or do you frequently find yourself interrupting them or finishing off their sentences for them?

    a. I usually let them finish
    b. I suppose that occasionally I may interrupt them or finish off what they are saying
    c. I admit that I do frequently interrupt or finish off their sentences for them

12. Which of the following words best describes you?
    a. dependent
    b. average
    c. important

13. Do you tend to sulk or play up if you don't get your own way?
    a. I hope not
    b. Maybe on occasions
    c. I have to say that I do

14. If you miss a telephone call and call 1471 for the number, do you always phone that number back to see what the caller wanted?
    a. Not usually, unless it is someone I really want to speak to or they are returning my call
    b. Only occasionally, and then only if I recognize the number
    c. Yes, I almost always call the number back whether I recognize the number or not

15. Would you call yourself a faddish eater?
    a. No
    b. No, but others have called me a faddish eater on occasions
    c. If that means having the willpower to give up something I enjoy eating, because it might not be organically good for me, then yes, I am a faddish eater

16. Are you interested in finding out as much as you can about all the people you know?
    a. Not particularly
    b. Not particularly, although I do join in the gossip from time to time
    c. Yes

17. Do you spend a lot of time on your appearance?

    a.   Not really

    b.   Not a lot of time, but I do take pride in my appearance

    c.   Yes, the way I appear and the way people see me is very important to me

18. Have you ever played matchmaker?

    a.   Never

    b.   Once

    c.   More than once

19. Do you prefer to hold a dinner party or to be invited to one?

    a.   Invited

    b.   No preference

    c.   Hold

20. You are carefree and single and see someone you are very attracted to at a party. Which of the following would you prefer to happen before the end of the evening?

    a.   Chat to them and eventually exchange phone numbers

    b.   Ask them out for a date, or be asked out for a date in the near future

    c.   Invite them to 'your place or mine' that same evening

21. Do you believe in the old adage 'If you want a job doing, do it yourself'?

    a.   Not really, that's too cynical for me

    b.   Sometimes

    c.   Usually, yes

22. Do you believe in pre-nuptial agreements?

    a.   No, it's a silly modern trend

    b.   Only for the very rich and famous perhaps

    c.   Yes

23. Do you ever feel stressed because you are not in control?
    a.   Never or rarely
    b.   Occasionally
    c.   More than occasionally

24. Do you want your partner to get to the top in his/her chosen vocation?
    a.   I only want for them what they would want for themselves
    b.   I wouldn't push them, but if they do well for themselves I am pleased for them
    c.   Yes, I am keen for my partner to become successful in their chosen vocation

25. Are you generally satisfied with your lot in life?
    a.   Yes
    b.   Fairly satisfied
    c.   No, I aspire for more

Analysis

Control is something most of us long for in our lives, and many of us will go to great lengths to achieve it. However, some will go to much greater lengths than others. There are many ways in which control-freakery can manifest itself, whether it is being fussy or over-fussy in the type of food we eat, controlling the way we look, even sometimes to the extent of undergoing plastic surgery, and planning ahead for all eventualities, by even, sometimes, making pre-nuptial agreements. For many people, having more control, not just over their own lives but of those around them, means they feel less stress, although this can have the reverse effect if and when it is brought home to them how little in fact they do control.

The following are a few of the telltale signs that you may be, or aspire to be, a control freak:

- a desire for knowledge, especially about other people – knowledge is power;
- a desire to dominate others, especially your partner;
- being very faddish about the food you eat, and having the self-control to maintain your strict eating habits;
- an enthusiasm to host dinner parties;
- you are something of a matchmaker;
- extremely fussy about your appearance;
- a desire to control the spending habits of your partner.

In general, the control freak has a need to be in control, and this could mean a fear of not being in control. In extreme cases, this fear could manifest itself in the need to try to control people with sarcasm or even bullying.

Assessment

Award yourself 2 points for every 'c' answer, 1 point for every 'b' and 0 points for every 'a'.

36–50 points

Your score does suggest that you are to a certain degree a control freak. Whilst this may mean that you feel in control of your life and thus not so prone to stress as many others, it may be necessary to curb these tendencies somewhat before you become too obsessed with imposing your own desires, tastes and lifestyle on the world around you; in other words, before your desire to be in charge gets out of hand.

Although it is great to be in charge of our own lives, do remember that life is also a team game where we depend to a very great extent on the help, love, respect and friendship of others for our own happiness. We cannot expect the world to revolve around us; therefore, it is often necessary to go with the flow.

21–35 points

You are in the happy position of being neither a control freak, nor someone who is likely to be over-dominated by others. It is likely that one of your chief priorities is to live in harmony with others and that you hold the belief that two heads are better than one, also that a problem shared is a problem halved, and that joint decisions are much more effective than those reached unilaterally.

Less than 20 points

You are most certainly not a control freak; in fact, just the reverse. This means that in the main you are likely to have a relaxed attitude towards life in general and are happy to go with the flow. The only problem is that you could be susceptible to being controlled, or even dominated by others. You should ensure, therefore, that your behaviour is not manipulated by others and remember at all times that you are your own person, and that the way you live and plan your life is ultimately your own decision.

8

Forward-looking, or stuck in a time warp

1. Do you like to keep abreast with the latest technology?
   a. Not particularly
   b. To a certain extent
   c. Yes

2. Do you constantly seek new hobbies and ventures?
   a. Not really, as any hobbies I have are things that I have been involved in, and have interested me, for many years
   b. Not particularly, although the occasional new interest may present itself to me
   c. Yes, I believe that every so often you just move onto new things

3. Do you go to new holiday places each year?
   a. No, I usually go to the same place each year
   b. Not each year as we have a few different favourite places that we like to alternate between
   c. Usually

4. Which of these is the most important to you?

    a. The past
    b. The present
    c. The future

5. Do you tend to hoard things?

    a. Yes
    b. Perhaps
    c. No

6. Which of these most closely represents your thoughts on 1 January?

    a. Here goes, another annus horribilis
    b. It doesn't seem anything like 12 months since last 1 January
    c. What new projects have I got planned for this year?

7. Do you believe there ever comes a time in life when you should just grow old gracefully?

    a. Yes
    b. Perhaps
    c. No

8. Is there a particular era in the past where they played your kind of music?

    a. Most certainly
    b. Perhaps I do like music of a certain era better than today's stuff
    c. No

9. Do you own a PC?

    a. No, and I have no plans to
    b. No, but I hope to own one in the future
    c. Yes

10. Would fond memories of living happily in the same home for many years prevent you from moving onto pastures new if you had the opportunity?

    a. Yes

    b. It would depend very much on what the pastures new were

    c. No

11. Which of the following is most important to you?

    a. A content and stable family life

    b. Live life to the full

    c. Continually expand your mind to its full potential

12. When you spend an evening with your nearest and dearest would you prefer to reminisce, or plan for the future?

    a. Reminisce

    b. Both equally

    c. Plan for the future

13. If someone does you a particularly bad turn, do you ever forgive them entirely?

    a. No

    b. Not until I have evened the score with them

    c. Forget them, rather than forgive

14. Do you have your own web page?

    a. No

    b. No, but I wouldn't rule out having one in the future

    c. Yes

15. Have your idols/heroes remained the same through the years?

    a.   Yes

    b.   Yes, although I have some modern idols/heroes too

    c.   No

16. Does the thought of new and seemingly complicated technology frighten you?

    a.   Yes

    b.   More overwhelms and confuses me than frightens me

    c.   Not frighten me, but sometimes I cannot rest until I have got to grips with it

17. Which of these most closely represents your attitude to change?

    a.   I hate change

    b.   I don't particularly like change but accept its inevitability

    c.   Change does not worry me in the slightest

18. Do you prefer to watch repeats of vintage programmes on television rather than new programmes?

    a.   Yes

    b.   Sometimes

    c.   No

19. What do you think about new fashions in clothing?

    a.   Not much

    b.   Some new fashions are OK, I suppose

    c.   Much of it is not for me but I like seeing people in new fashions providing it suits them

20. How easily are you able to move on from personal tragedy?

    a.   Not at all easily; in fact, it is a very long and difficult process

    b.   I try to move on in time, although no one fully recovers from a serious personal tragedy or bereavement

    c.   It is not easy. However, I do try to put it behind me and get on with the rest of my life as quickly as possible

21. Do you ever visit your old haunts to invoke happy memories and renew old acquaintances?

    a.   More than occasionally

    b.   Occasionally

    c.   Never or rarely

22. Which of the following do you consider to be your greatest strength?

    a.   Organized

    b.   Responsible

    c.   Energetic

23. How do you feel about the company you work for constantly introducing all the latest technology?

    a.   Somewhat apprehensive as I feel much more comfortable with what I know

    b.   I realize it is necessary in today's world in order to remain competitive, but sometimes I worry that I will not be able to adapt to the new technology

    c.   I welcome it unreservedly as an exciting new challenge

24. Do you think your schooldays were the happiest days of your life?

    a. Yes
    b. Not particularly, although I do have some fond memories of my schooldays
    c. No

25. Have you ever mastered an item of new technology to the extent that you have shown someone else how to use it?

    a. No
    b. Occasionally
    c. More than occasionally

Assessment

Award yourself 2 points for every 'c' answer, 1 point for every 'b', and 0 points for every 'a'

40–50 points

You would appear to be someone who is extremely forward-looking and not in any way stuck in a time warp. What this means is that you are likely to be continually looking forward to, and planning for, the future, whatever your age. Change for you is something that need not necessarily be a bad thing; in fact, you are excited by the plans you are continually making and excited about some of the opportunities the future may bring.

You are also keenly interested in new technology and have a desire to be involved in any new developments that are taking place and not get left behind. Of course, technological change is now taking place at such a rapid rate that most of us are at least one step behind with the latest gadgets or innovations, so you should not feel frustrated if you suddenly discover that some latest development has escaped your attention, or that the computer you bought six months ago is suddenly no longer the most powerful model. Your philosophy is that you should never go back, and that in life we should be continually moving forward irrespective of age.

25–39 points

Our past memories and experiences make us what we are today. It is these experiences that enable us to live for today and give us a foundation on which to build for the future. Whilst your score does indicate that you are forward-looking and like to make plans for the future, and keep abreast with the latest technology, you are also fond of your memories and of times past. You are in the happy position of not being afraid of change and the new challenges and new technology that change inevitably brings. You remain optimistic for the future but at the same time somewhat nostalgic for times past.

Less than 25 points

Oscar Wilde once said that there were two things in life that were certain: death and taxes. Had he been alive today I suspect he would have added a third – change. Change has always been inevitable, but today changes in lifestyle, attitudes and technology mean that this change is taking place at an even greater rate than ever before. We can either resist this change, in which case we tend to get stuck in a time warp, or we embrace change and move forward with it.

It would appear that you are quite resistant to change and not particularly interested in moving forward at the rate this change is occurring. The indications are also that you are not particularly interested in new technology, but this may be because you find the prospect of getting to grips with it somewhat overwhelming.

Because you tend to look back at what you considered the better times, you are probably something of a sentimentalist. The time in your life that you look back on the most is likely to be a particular era when a change in your life occurred for the better. If, however, you change your philosophy just a little and consider the good things that are happening right now, this will give you more encouragement to look forward to the future with a more optimistic outlook, and you may then find that the pattern will repeat itself, and in years to come you look back on the current era with the same degree of sentimentality that you have now for times past.

Also, remember that we, all of us, are never too old to learn. Whilst technological advances are taking place at a rapid rate, in the majority of cases these technological advances are made for the purpose of enriching our lives, and we can either be part of this life-enriching process, or we can ignore it and not reap the benefits it provides.

9

How soft-centred are you?

1. Which of the following most closely represents your opinion of St Valentine's Day?

    a. A day when people who are falling in love or dating buy each other cards and presents
    b. A romantic day when you always buy your loved one a card and a present
    c. A day when people make a quick buck selling cards, flowers and chocolates at inflated prices

2. Which of the following is your favourite type of music?

    a. Anything as long as it is lively and has a beat
    b. Romantic music, be it jazz, classical or pop
    c. Anything as long as it is loud and brassy or stirring

3. After an argument with your partner would you buy them a gift to make it up, even though you did not believe it was you that was at fault?

    a. Maybe
    b. Yes
    c. No way

4. If your work colleague was on a final warning for careless work, would you take the blame for them to prevent them from being sacked after yet another error?

    a. It would all depend. Perhaps so if they were also one of my close friends and/or they had a partner and family to support
    b. Yes
    c. No

5. Do you feel sorry for beggars in the street?

    a. Yes
    b. Yes, and I often give them money
    c. No

6. Would you ever give a stray dog or cat a home?

    a. I think that I would if the situation ever arose
    b. Yes, in fact it is something that I have done
    c. I very much doubt that I would

7. It is a very busy time at work and you are up to your eyes in important paperwork and a demanding schedule. Under those circumstances would you take a couple of days off to spend some much-needed quality time with your partner?

    a. Yes, but I wouldn't really be at ease with the thought of all that work on my mind, so under the circumstances it wouldn't really be quality time
    b. Yes
    c. No, it would be irresponsible to leave my important work undone under the circumstances and I would hope that my partner would understand

8. Do you always tell your partner about any of their habits that you find annoying?

   a. Occasionally
   b. Never or very rarely
   c. More than occasionally

9. You have booked tickets to see your favourite pop star who you have been waiting to see live for years. Then a close friend asks you to help out at a charity event they have organized. You know that they have taken too much on and have no one else to turn to. What would you do?

   a. Tell your friend you will help them out if it is absolutely necessary but also explain about your plans to see the pop concert
   b. Help them out and cancel your visit to the pop concert, and not even tell your friend you had something else planned
   c. Under the circumstances I could not miss the once-in-a-lifetime opportunity to see my favourite pop star

10. Your partner seems tired and preoccupied about something. How do you react?

    a. Say nothing immediately, but after a day or so, if they appear no better ask them if they are feeling OK
    b. Tell them you are worried about them and ask if everything is OK
    c. Say nothing in the belief they will soon snap out of it

11. If you saw someone fall full length in a crowded street, how would you react?

    a. Watch to make sure they get up and walk on or that someone nearer than you goes to their assistance
    b. I would instinctively run to their aid
    c. Probably do nothing but hope they are OK

12. Do you usually feel sorry for the underdog?

    a.   Sometimes

    b.   Usually

    c.   Not particularly

13. Have you ever written someone a love letter?

    a.   Occasionally

    b.   More than occasionally

    c.   Rarely or never

14. What would be your idea of the perfect romantic evening in with someone you were dating?

    a.   A meal, a sexy movie and some intimate passion for afters

    b.   A meal, comfortable sofa and a slushy movie

    c.   Supper and breakfast

15. Do you often buy your partner presents?

    a.   Not often, but I never forget birthdays and Christmas

    b.   Yes, I like to surprise my partner with presents whenever I can

    c.   Not as often as I should

16. Do you feel sorry for celebrities who are being vilified in the press?

    a.   Occasionally

    b.   More than occasionally

    c.   Never or rarely

17. How easy is it for you to say no when asked for a favour?

    a.   I have no problem if I feel the favour being asked is an impossible one or is unreasonable

    b.   Difficult

    c.   Not difficult

18. Late at night you turn on the news channel and hear about a little dog trapped down a well, which a team of firefighters is trying to rescue. Which of the following would most apply to you the following morning?

   a.   You would probably go about your usual routine, but might remember the story sometime during the day and mention it to a work colleague or acquaintance to see if they had heard whether it had been rescued

   b.   The dog would be on your mind so much that you would tune into the news channel as soon as you got up, to try to find out if it had been rescued

   c.   Probably do nothing as you would have forgotten all about it

19. How often do you tell someone some home truths?

   a.   Occasionally
   b.   Never or rarely
   c.   More than occasionally

20. Have you ever found tears streaming down your face when watching a sad movie or something sad on television?

   a.   On rare occasions
   b.   More than on rare occasions
   c.   No

21. Have you ever cried with emotion because you felt so happy for someone other than yourself?

   a.   Only on very rare occasions
   b.   More than on very rare occasions
   c.   No

22. Which of the following qualities do you think is most essential for a successful long-term relationship?
    a. A good family life
    b. Caring and sharing
    c. Dynamic and continually stimulating

23. Which of the following represents your immediate reaction when first seeing breaking news footage on television of a heinous act of terrorism?
    a. Feelings of anger and outrage at the perpetrators
    b. Great sorrow for the innocent victims and their families
    c. A feeling of 'there but for the grace of God go I'

24. Have you ever found tears streaming down your face because of the emotion of watching a movie or something on television with a wonderfully happy ending?
    a. Occasionally
    b. More than occasionally
    c. Never

25. Do you believe your heart rules your head or your head rules your heart?
    a. Both equally
    b. Heart rules head
    c. Head rules heart

Assessment

Award yourself 2 points for every 'b' answer, 1 point for every 'a' and 0 points for every 'c'.

40–50 points

You are an extremely romantic and caring person and you are often deeply touched by the feelings of others, and affected by news bulletins highlighting the plight of others, to the extent that you often feel guilty that you are not out there helping them in some way. Because you are such a soft-centred and caring person this does mean that you are liked and respected by others. However, it also means that sometimes you may be taken advantage of, especially if you find it difficult, almost impossible, to say no.

Keywords: romantic, caring, soft-hearted, idealistic

25–39 points

Whilst you are generally a soft-centred person who would go to great lengths not to hurt other people's feelings, it may be that there is a need to peel off one or two layers before this soft centre is revealed. The advantage of this is that you are still tough enough to realize your ambitions whilst retaining the loving and caring side of your personality. Like a great many people you are a real softy at heart.

Keywords: loving, empathetic, confident

Less than 25 points

Whilst your score does indicate that you are more of a hard nut than someone who is soft-centred, it may be that beneath this apparent hard exterior there lies something of a soft centre. It may be that this apparent hard exterior is, in fact, something of an act because you do not wish to be perceived as being soft, or display weakness.

At the same time, you cannot in any way be described as a romantic or sentimentalist. However, this does not stop you from having a long and loving relationship and secure family life, and people will respect you and take you for what you are, and admire your honesty.

Whilst you do not lack honesty, it may be beneficial, not just for yourself, but for those around you, to always keep in mind the feelings of others and to try to empathize with them.

Keywords: pragmatic, dispassionate, taciturn

10

Attitude

In each of the following, choose from a scale of 1–5 which of these statements you most agree with or is most applicable to you. Choose just one of the numbers 1–5 in each of the 25 statements. Choose 5 for most agree/most applicable, down to 1 for least agree/least applicable.

1. I am proud of my nationality

   5   4   3   2   1

2. I would tell a shopkeeper if I noticed his/her shop was selling food beyond its sell-by-date

   5   4   3   2   1

3. Parents should teach their children the difference between right and wrong from a very early age

   5   4   3   2   1

4. People are basically decent

   5   4   3   2   1

5. I continually look forward to, and plan for, the future

    5   4   3   2   1

6. I try not to react to different people in different ways no matter what their status or authority

    5   4   3   2   1

7. The more knowledge and information we each learn about the world and its people in general, the better and safer the world will become

    5   4   3   2   1

8. I am extremely worried about the level of crime and violence in our society

    5   4   3   2   1

9. I believe in the basic principle that 'the customer is always right'

    5   4   3   2   1

10. There are very few people I know that I would not trust

    5   4   3   2   1

11. I forgive and forget as quickly as possible

    5   4   3   2   1

12. I am always frank and candid about who I am and what I believe in

    5   4   3   2   1

13. I channel all my energies into making a good job of what I
    am doing

    5   4   3   2   1

14. I am happy when others like and respect me

    5   4   3   2   1

15. I am angry when people or groups of people become stereo-
    typed

    5   4   3   2   1

16. I try to understand the other person's point of view

    5   4   3   2   1

17. I do not tend to complain a lot

    5   4   3   2   1

18. I am eager to please others

    5   4   3   2   1

19. It is unusual for me to stand or walk with my hands in my
    pockets

    5   4   3   2   1

20. I am anxious to learn about the beliefs of other people

    5   4   3   2   1

21. I strive to keep myself fit and in good shape

    5   4   3   2   1

22. In general we make our own luck

    5   4   3   2   1

23. I smile more than most other people I know

    5   4   3   2   1

24. I keep a tidy house and garden at all times

    5   4   3   2   1

25. On first meeting someone I make a conscious effort not to judge that person by his/her appearance

    5   4   3   2   1

Analysis

Nobody is born with an attitude. Attitudes are formed in many different ways, for example having direct experience with people and events, and the influences in our lives, such as parents, with whom many people hold the same beliefs. Our attitude is something that is noticed by other people more than ourselves. In many cases, a person's attitude is a natural attribute formed by that person's personality. It is, however, very wide-ranging, and very difficult to define.

Originally the term is derived from the Latin *aptitudo*, meaning 'fitness', thus, rendering one fit to engage in the performance of a particular task. Another definition of attitude is the explanation of the actions of a person due to how that person feels about something, for example consciously held beliefs or opinions and emotional feelings.

An individual's attitude can also change due to changes in circumstances or stimuli, and these changes can either be positive – a better attitude – or negative – a worse attitude. Sometimes, attempts at changing the attitude of an individual may work, or they may have the reverse effect, in which the attitude is changed but in an opposite direction to that intended.

Social psychologists have identified several ways in which attitudes are used by individuals:

- One of these ways is known as the knowledge function, where attitudes are used to organize mentally all the knowledge we have amassed about the world, and the using of information in this way can help us to make more sense of the world.
- Another is the value-expressive function, the function we are all perhaps most familiar with, which refers to the use of attitudes to express one's values. In this way your attitudes will reveal to others who and what you are, and what you believe in.
- The third basic way in which attitudes are used by individuals is called the utilitarian/instrumental function and this is the method by which we obtain rewards and avoid punishment.
- Finally, there is the ego-defensive function, whereby attitude is used to help defend self-image or ego. Someone, for example, who feels inadequate in the workplace may try to make someone else appear more inadequate or inferior as a way of shielding his or her own feelings of inadequacy from the scrutiny of others.

Assessment

Total score 90–125

You have a very good attitude to life in general. This means that you are not only positive, but also enthusiastic about all the tasks you undertake. This positive attitude is noticed by others, and will stand you in good stead both in your business and private life. There is no need for change.

Total score 65–89

Whilst your score means you have, in the main, the right attitude, there may still be room for improvement. Even though you do not have an attitude problem, far from it, it may be a useful exercise from time to time to carry out a self-analysis to consider not just your attitude to any tasks you perform, but also your attitude to others in our society and the wider world.

Total score less than 65

Attitude is increasingly important in modern living. When we go into a shop we expect the person behind the counter to be not only enthusiastic and knowledgeable about the product he or she is selling, but also to go out of his or her way to be helpful and to be anxious to please the customer. The keyword here is enthusiasm, and it is this enthusiasm for living that the person with the right attitude will convey to others.

Your score indicates that in certain, but not necessarily all, respects you may have an attitude problem, and it may therefore be worth analysing your score on the individual questions within this test, especially where you have indicated a score of 3 or less. It is in these areas that perhaps your attitude needs to be considered and worked upon.

As our attitudes are often formed by external influences it may be worth considering whether such influences are present, and if these influences are negative, how they can be changed so that your negative attitude can be reversed. The more we understand about our own attitudes and beliefs, the more chance we have of changing our negative attitudes to more positive ones.

11

Optimist or pessimist?

1. Do you ever worry, for the future generation, about what the world will be like in 50 years' time?

   a. More than occasionally
   b. Very rarely or never
   c. Occasionally

2. If you break a mirror, how concerned are you that it will bring bad luck?

   a. Quite concerned
   b. Not concerned in the slightest
   c. Slightly concerned

3. When you take part in any sort of contest, do you expect to win?

   a. Not usually
   b. Yes, I usually expect to win
   c. I like to win, but realize that I will sometimes come out second best

4. How often have you chased your losses at gambling?

    a. Never
    b. More than once or twice
    c. Perhaps once or twice

5. Do you believe that in life there is the ideal partner for everyone?

    a. Only in fairy stories
    b. Yes
    c. Some people, but not everyone

6. Do you consider that your cup of life is half full, or half empty?

    a. Half empty
    b. Half full
    c. Neither

7. How would you complete the saying: 'If at first you don't succeed...

    a. Give up
    b. Try again
    c. Try, try and try again

8. Do you always feel that it will be possible to achieve your goals in life?

    a. Less than usually
    b. Yes
    c. Usually

9. Do you agree that every dog has its day?

    a. Disagree
    b. Strongly agree
    c. Partly agree

10. After adversity, how quickly are you able to pick yourself up and dust yourself down?

    a. Not very quickly
    b. Almost immediately
    c. Fairly quickly

11. How often do you lose sleep through worrying?

    a. More than occasionally
    b. Rarely or never
    c. Occasionally

12. How confident are you usually that you have made the correct decision when faced with a choice?

    a. Not at all confident
    b. Usually fairly confident
    c. I worry about it a little perhaps

13. If you had a bad dose of flu would you see the doctor?

    a. Probably
    b. No
    c. Doubtful

14. Do you believe in keeping your aspirations low, so as to avoid disappointment?

    a. Yes
    b. No
    c. Sometimes

15. Do you feel secure financially?

    a. No
    b. Yes
    c. Most of the time

16. Do you believe that when one door closes another opens?
    a.   No, life is not that simple
    b.   Yes
    c.   Sometimes

17. Do you believe that your friends will never let you down?
    a.   Unfortunately not
    b.   Yes, usually
    c.   Not sure

18. Is it your philosophy that there will always be calm after the storm, or storm after the calm?
    a.   Storm after the calm
    b.   Calm after the storm
    c.   Both, as life is full of ups and downs

19. How long does it take you to count your blessings?
    a.   Not long
    b.   I could almost go on forever counting them
    c.   About the same time as most other people I suppose

20. Which of these song titles/adages is most applicable to your general outlook on life?
    a.   'The other person's grass is always greener'
    b.   'Every cloud has a silver lining'
    c.   'Somewhere over the rainbow, bluebirds fly'

21. Do you expect to live to a ripe old age?
    a.   Not particularly
    b.   Yes
    c.   I hope so

22. Do you believe your next big break is just around the corner?

    a.   Big breaks don't just happen, they have to be created
    b.   Yes
    c.   Hopefully

23. Would you take out a large mortgage, confident you would be able to make the repayments?

    a.   I might, but it would worry me greatly
    b.   Yes
    c.   Yes, but it would worry me somewhat

24. Do you believe that bad news always comes in threes?

    a.   Usually
    b.   If it does, then it is always balanced out when good news comes in threes
    c.   It does sometimes

25. Do you worry about flying?

    a.   Usually
    b.   Rarely or never
    c.   Sometimes

26. Do you believe there is an afterlife?

    a.   No
    b.   Yes
    c.   I hope there is but I am not sure

27. When you buy a lottery ticket or scratch card, do you expect to win?

    a.   Not really
    b.   Yes, I wouldn't buy one otherwise
    c.   I am hopeful, but also realistic about my chances

28. Do you believe in the ultimate triumph of good over evil?
    a. Not really, especially in today's troubled world
    b. Yes, good will always triumph over evil, that is why we are all still here
    c. Not sure

29. If you were stranded on a desert island, how would you rate your chances of being rescued?
    a. I would probably resign myself to never being rescued, but retain that slight glimmer of hope
    b. I would know in my heart of hearts that one day I would be rescued
    c. I would just hope for the best and try to survive in the meantime

30. How often have you applied to become a contestant on a quiz show with aspirations of winning loads-a-money?
    a. Never
    b. More than occasionally
    c. Occasionally

Assessment

Award yourself 2 points for every 'b' answer, 1 point for every 'c' and 0 points for every 'a'.

45–60 points

You appear to be the eternal optimist with a wonderful outlook on life, the modern-day Mr Micawber who is always expecting something to turn up! Not for you sleepless nights worrying about things that may never happen; instead, you tend to look on the bright side whatever happens and firmly believe that every cloud has a silver lining. As long as you do not become naive about life's sometimes harsh realities, then you will remain cheerful, to a great extent carefree, and happy in the confident belief that you can get the best out of life, but at the same time being well prepared to accept the inevitable ups and downs.

27–44 points

Like most people in this world you are a realist. You realize that life is a roller coaster, but roller coaster rides can be quite exciting and stimulating, and hopefully the high points will exceed the low points, and this is what really counts in the end.

Although you do not appear to be a pessimist, perhaps something to be learned from the eternal optimist is that we should not worry so much. Remember that most of the things that we do worry about in life never happen anyway, so why worry about them until they actually do happen?

Less than 27 points

Although you might describe yourself as a realist, you appear to be a born pessimist. While this does not make you a worse person, and you can still be successful and make many friends, it does mean that you are probably seen by others as a negative person, and that you suffer from a great deal of inner turmoil and unnecessary sleepless nights. It may be that this is a way of creating your own defensive shield against the consequences of what the future may bring. If it turns out better than expected then you will feel good, but if it turns out badly you will not feel let down, as you have already prepared yourself for the worst. In actual fact, having such a negative attitude does not make things any better or worse in the end, but in some cases, worry about the future can lead to stress-related illness and make negative things happen that wouldn't otherwise.

What you must try to do is not make mountains out of mole-hills. Instead, try to put negative thoughts to the back of your mind. Try instead to think of the positive aspects of your life. If you can do this, and admittedly it is easier said than done and may take a great deal of effort on your part, you will start to reap the benefits, not just in your well-being and state of health, but by an improved outlook on life in general.

12

Are you a good team player?

In each of the following, rank the four statements in each group according to which is most applicable to you, which is least applicable, and which of the remaining two are next most applicable and next least applicable.

1.

a. In each team there should be someone in charge or overall control

b. It is more important for team members to have their own defined areas of responsibility than to have someone in overall control

c. The best team leaders create the conditions necessary to motivate their team

d. The best team leaders have the charisma necessary to motivate their team

2.

a. A team can only be at its strongest when its purpose is in line with all its members' wants and needs
b. A team is at its strongest when it is working well within itself
c. A team is at its strongest when clear objectives are set
d. A team is at its strongest when the objectives set may at first glance seem too difficult to achieve

3.

a. I will channel all my energies into fulfilling all the needs and objectives of my team
b. I am ambitious and will channel a great deal of my energies into becoming team leader
c. One of the greatest motivators is responding to a challenge
d. I aspire to be team leader

4.

a. The best team leaders have the ability of helping others to see the best in themselves
b. The most effective team leaders are those who take a back seat as long as the team is working efficiently, and only become involved when something goes wrong
c. A good leader should encourage a feeling of camaraderie between the team members
d. A good leader is a catalyst for motivation

5.

a. Teams and team members are stimulated by being given responsibility
b. Team members should be aware of the consequences of making errors
c. Teams should never be afraid of making changes
d. Team members should continually analyse and appraise each other

6.

a. I believe the team will be better off as a result of my participation

b. Team members should be equally adept at doing any job within the team

c. It is important I am there to assist all my fellow team members at all times

d. Regular team meetings are essential in order to evaluate performance and reappraise goals

Analysis

A keyword in building a good team is motivation, and a key question to be asked is 'What makes us do anything?' There are several factors to be addressed when considering what will constitute a good team and who will make a good team member. Some of these factors can be summarized as follows.

What is the purpose of the team?

Motivation could be lacking if the purpose of the team is not clearly defined and is not in line with the needs of some team members. It is often said that a team is only as strong as its weakest link.

Who will be my fellow team members?

Camaraderie is a key factor in building a successful team. It encourages openness, communication, fellowship and loyalty. A team is at its most effective when its members are all pulling together in the same direction. A team should be well balanced and bring together all the different kinds of human skills and technical expertise necessary in fulfilling a particular task.

Will the work be something that is of particular interest to me?

Team members need to feel that the work is important and that the mission is clear. Their interest and motivation will diminish if the aims of the team are not in line with their own aspirations.

What challenges does the team face?

People either respond to challenge in a positive way, or walk away from it. In general, a challenge has the effect of motivating a team and helps them to pull together and respond to the challenge. The greater the challenge, the greater the effort. Challenge, therefore, is in itself a motivator.

Even though difficulties will occur and from time to time some members' needs and attitudes will change, and there will be some changes in personnel, if the members of the team are working towards these common purposes then motivation should be sustained over a long period.

Assessment

Scoring instructions: place a tick in the appropriate column for each letter.

Group	Most	Next most	Next least	Least	Score
1.					
a.	☐	☐	☐	☐	☐
b.	☐	☐	☐	☐	☐
c.	☐	☐	☐	☐	☐
d.	☐	☐	☐	☐	☐

2.
a. ☐ ☐ ☐ ☐ ☐
b. ☐ ☐ ☐ ☐ ☐
c. ☐ ☐ ☐ ☐ ☐
d. ☐ ☐ ☐ ☐ ☐

3.
a. ☐ ☐ ☐ ☐ ☐
b. ☐ ☐ ☐ ☐ ☐
c. ☐ ☐ ☐ ☐ ☐
d. ☐ ☐ ☐ ☐ ☐

4.
a. ☐ ☐ ☐ ☐ ☐
b. ☐ ☐ ☐ ☐ ☐
c. ☐ ☐ ☐ ☐ ☐
d. ☐ ☐ ☐ ☐ ☐

5.
a. ☐ ☐ ☐ ☐ ☐
b. ☐ ☐ ☐ ☐ ☐
c. ☐ ☐ ☐ ☐ ☐
d. ☐ ☐ ☐ ☐ ☐

6.
a. ☐ ☐ ☐ ☐ ☐
b. ☐ ☐ ☐ ☐ ☐
c. ☐ ☐ ☐ ☐ ☐
d. ☐ ☐ ☐ ☐ ☐

Score 3 points for every 'a' answer ticked in Most, 2 points for every 'a' answer ticked in Next most, 1 point for every 'a' answer ticked in Next least and 0 points for every 'a' answer ticked in Least.

Score 0 points for every 'b' answer ticked in Most, 1 point for every 'b' answer ticked in Next most, 2 points for every 'b' answer ticked in Next least and 3 points for every 'b' answer ticked in Least.

Score 2 points for every 'c' answer ticked in Most, 3 points for every 'c' answer ticked in Next most, 1 point for every 'c' answer ticked in Next least and 0 points for every 'c' answer ticked in Least.

Score 0 points for every 'd' answer ticked in Most, 1 point for every 'd' answer ticked in Next most, 3 points for every 'd' answer ticked in Next least and 2 points for every 'd' answer ticked in Least.

48–72 points

Not only are you a good team player, but you have a clear understanding of what makes a good team player, and how to get the best out of a team, and as a result you should make a good team leader, if you are not one already.

A good leader is required to understand the importance of the team's purpose and challenges but also needs to focus on maintaining its camaraderie, responsibility and growth. The best team leaders are able to create the right conditions in which the team is able to motivate itself. If you are a team player, but not already a leader, then perhaps you should set your aspirations somewhat higher, but only if that is what you really want from life.

24–47 points

You are likely to prove a good team player with possible leadership qualities. Both teams and individuals are stimulated by responsibility and you are likely to possess the right attitude to take these responsibilities seriously and to recognize the need for team members to pull together to achieve their objectives. Whilst a team does consist of individuals, it is only when these individuals pull together as a team towards a common goal that the team can really be effective.

23 points or less

It does appear that you are more of an individual than a team player and, as such, prefer tasks where you are working on your own. You also probably prefer taking part in individual sports, rather than team games.

It may be that you do not like the interference of others, or that you do not like working under a team leader or captain, or that you are somewhat resentful of people who are put in charge when, perhaps, you feel you could do a better job. Or perhaps you do not particularly like people in positions of authority. Your score does, therefore, suggest that you will be most suited to a job or profession where you are allowed to work on your own, with as little interference and interaction from others as possible. It should, however, always be borne in mind that life is to a great extent a team game, and that cooperation is always more productive than confrontation or isolationism. Team growth can also lead to individual growth in which we can all move forward by learning new concepts, increasing our skills, broadening our minds and sustaining motivation.

13

How assertive are you?

1. You are a member of a committee and the position of chair suddenly becomes vacant. What is your reaction?

   a. I would be keen to fill the vacant position if I was asked
   b. I would do everything possible to try to be elected to the vacant position
   c. I would consider standing for election to the vacant position but only if asked to do so

2. Do you believe that compromise is the best way to solve a problem?

   a. Yes, but it must be a workable compromise that meets everyone's needs to some extent
   b. Not if it means giving way to demands that are unreasonable, or that I strongly disagree with
   c. Yes, as compromise is sometimes the only way forward

3. Which of the following is most important to you?

   a. The right to live in peace and harmony
   b. The right to say no
   c. The right to be treated fairly at all times

4. Your new work colleague, whom you have not had time to get to know very well, asks to borrow £50 to pay a bill as he or she has a temporary cash flow problem. How are you likely to handle this situation?

    a. Explain tactfully that you do not lend money to work colleagues
    b. I would have no problem refusing his or her request
    c. I would probably agree just this once so as not to jeopardize my future working relationship with him/her

5. You are in a queue and someone pushes in front of you. How would you react?

    a. Make a tutting noise, or some other reaction, to make them aware you are annoyed about it
    b. I would tell the person to get to the back of the queue
    c. I would feel annoyed but probably do nothing

6. Do you ever find yourself being easily manipulated?

    a. Sometimes
    b. No
    c. Yes

7. You are in a shop and on the way out realize you have been short-changed by a very small amount. What is your reaction?

    a. Tell the assistant you have been short-changed but accept their reaction
    b. Point out the mistake and insist on getting the correct change
    c. Let it go as you feel that going back would be too much hassle

8. Which of the following is most important in your working environment?

    a. Car parking facilities
    b. Flexitime
    c. Good canteen facilities

9. How confident would you be at expressing your viewpoint at a meeting even though you know a large majority of people present will not agree with you?

    a. Not very confident but may pluck up the courage to put my viewpoint forward anyway
    b. Relish the situation as I am very confident of my powers of persuasion
    c. Not very confident and would probably keep my thoughts to myself under the circumstances

10. How do you usually react to criticism?

    a. Dispute what they are saying
    b. Assess the criticism and respond appropriately rather than react to it
    c. Feel quite upset but accept that the person making the criticism is entitled to their opinion

11. What do you believe is most important in effective communication?

    a. Speed of response
    b. Keep it simple and keep it short
    c. Be polite and courteous at all times

12. You see some young children walking across the bottom of your garden. How are you likely to react?

    a. Say hello to them and make some remark such as 'Now what are you doing in my garden?', but in a friendly sort of way

b.   Point out to them gently but firmly that they are on private property

c.   Do nothing in the hope that it is just a one-off

13. You are in the non-smoking part of a restaurant and someone at the next table lights up a cigarette. Which of the following is most likely to be your reaction?

a.   Point it out to the restaurant staff on the assumption that they will tell the person they are in a non-smoking area

b.   Point out to them very politely that this is a non-smoking part of the restaurant

c.   Probably do nothing

14. Which of the following do you believe is the most important?

a.   Being tough with the person you are dealing with, and tough with the issue

b.   Being kind to people but tough with the issue

c.   Respecting the other person's viewpoint

15. A tradesperson comes to your house and charges what you believe to be a grossly excessive amount for just 15 minutes' work. Which of the following is most likely to be your reaction?

a.   Say 'Are you sure, it seems a lot?' However, if they insist, pay up reluctantly and put the episode down to experience

b.   Say that you do not feel able to pay what they have asked and tell them what you think would be a reasonable amount for the work carried out

c.   Say nothing but make a mental note not to use that person again.

16. Your boss asks you to complete a project to a deadline you feel is unreasonable and impossible. How are you most likely to handle this situation?

    a.   Reluctantly accept the deadline knowing that you may be late in completing

    b.   Try to convince your boss that you need more time in order to complete the project to the highest standard

    c.   Burn the midnight oil in order to complete the project on time and impress your boss

17. With which of the following do you most agree?

    a.   A problem shared is a problem halved

    b.   Ultimately you must find the solutions to your own problems

    c.   Most problems resolve themselves with time

18. Which of the following do you believe is most important in winning arguments?

    a.   To be able to give and take

    b.   To keep self-control

    c.   To know you are right

19. Which of the following is most applicable to you?

    a.   I let my opinions be known

    b.   I ask for what I want

    c.   I take into account the needs of others

20. Which of the following do you believe is the most effective way to start a sentence?

    a.   I feel...

    b.   I suggest...

    c.   I understand...

21. Which of the following words is most applicable to you?

    a. Patient
    b. Persistent
    c. Dependable

22. You are asked to plan a social event, but then someone else starts to take over, which undermines the work you are doing. How are you likely to handle this situation?

    a. Do nothing and put up with the situation
    b. Politely make it clear that it is you who has been asked to organize the event
    c. Suggest they take over the running of the event from you, if that's what they prefer

23. Which of the following words is most applicable to you?

    a. Emphatic
    b. Positive
    c. Impetuous

24. Do you accept yourself for what you are?

    a. Yes, as long as other people accept me
    b. Yes, with all my imperfections
    c. Not always

25. Which of the following do you believe to be the most effective in winning arguments?

    a. Do not continually interrupt the other party
    b. Stick to the point
    c. Be prepared to compromise

Analysis

One definition of assertiveness is the need to stand up for our own rights and aspirations in today's sometimes intimidating world. It is necessary for us all to possess basic assertiveness skills to see us through the day, in order to maintain our self-esteem and to provide a shield to protect ourselves. As a result of applying these basic skills we will feel better about ourselves, will recognize what we want, have the ability to say what we want, be able to apply the correct degree of persistence, will not leave ourselves subject to manipulation by others and we will have the ability to respond to criticism in an appropriate manner. We will thus have the ability to take more responsibility for what happens in our life and take more control of it by deciding what we require and keeping focused on what we want. At the same time we will be able to enjoy what we have already achieved and celebrate our successes.

Assertiveness is also knowing our own rights as individuals. These include having the right to ask for what we want, having the right to ask for what we need, having the right to make choices and having the right to say no. It is also having the right to be our own person and accept ourselves for what we are, including our imperfections.

In order for assertiveness to be effective it is necessary to hone our communication skills. This includes understanding exactly what we are asking for, as people will tend to treat us the way we ask to be treated. The most effective assertive communication is, therefore, based on respect for ourselves, and respect for others.

Self-respect means that how we handle situations affects our chances of success, and how we feel afterwards. It also means being in control and is not about winning every argument. If we lose control then it is almost certain that the argument is lost.

Assessment

Award yourself 2 points for every 'b' answer, 1 point for every 'a' and 0 points for every 'c'.

40–50 points

You come over as a very assertive person who knows their rights and is not afraid of knowing and saying what you want in any situation. There is no doubt that you believe that you are your own ultimate judge and each person must ultimately come to terms with the challenges of living by learning to cope on their own. This is fine just as long as you do not become too demanding a person, but retain compassion for the troubles of others and are capable of keeping your demands realistic. You should also ensure that your reaction to criticism is an appropriate one. If you react to criticism, rather than respond to it, this is a sure-fire way of losing the argument.

Remember at all times that some ways of asserting your demands are much more effective than others, and that it is impossible to win every single argument. If you feel the need to persist then stay calm at all times. It does not really matter how many times you hear the word 'no' in an argument, you only need one 'yes' for success. Often the word 'no', is merely a step on the way to hearing the word 'yes'. Remember that assertiveness skills do not win every time. However, assertive behaviour maintains self-respect and generally makes you feel better afterwards.

25–39 points

Your score indicates that you have the perfect balance of assertiveness skills required to maintain your self-esteem, to know your rights, to have the confidence to ask for these rights and, as a result, to feel good about yourself. You are able to adopt a positive attitude, be assertive when required, and generally feel happy about the way you have conducted yourself. You also have the ability of recognizing the importance, when the situation demands it, of finding a workable compromise that meets not just your aspirations, but also the aspirations of others.

Less than 25 points

Whilst you may know your rights, it appears you lack the necessary assertiveness not just to ask for these rights, or know how to ask in the most effective manner, but to say 'no'. It may be necessary to analyse your individual responses to the questions in this test in conjunction with the above analysis to try to find ways in which your basic assertiveness skills are not as effective as perhaps they should be. Remember that there is never any harm in asking. You will not hear the word 'yes' every time, but you will never hear the word 'yes' if you do not ask in the first place.

Bear in mind always that assertiveness means taking control of your communication and the way to create successful communication is by the use of direct, clear language, keeping things short and simple, keeping to the point, setting the scene and using silence where appropriate. It also means working on your listening skills – there is nothing more infuriating than being interrupted when you are in the middle of making a point, and it means fully understanding what the other person is saying even if that means asking them to clarify things. You should, therefore, at all times endeavour to create a good rapport with the other party and at all times strive to be kind to people even if you are tough with the issue.

14

How patient are you?

1. Do you believe in the old adage, 'Everything comes to he/she who waits'?

   a. Mostly, but occasionally it helps to push things along somewhat
   b. No way, the only thing certain to come to he/she who waits is death and taxes
   c. Yes, this generally proves to be the case

2. What is likely to be the outcome if you sit down to do a crossword puzzle?

   a. I usually complete all the answers that immediately spring to mind and after that give up
   b. It is very unlikely that I would ever even attempt a crossword puzzle
   c. I usually stick at it until I have completed or almost completed it

3. Do you like to work on one long, or difficult, project until it is completed?

    a. If possible, but sometimes I like to break off to do other things in order to refresh my mind
    b. Not really, I have a tendency to have many incomplete projects on the go at any one time
    c. Yes, that is what I prefer

4. How good are you, or were you, at revising for examinations?

    a. Not very good, I really have/had to force myself to put my mind to the task
    b. Terrible, I would have obtained much better exam results if I had revised more
    c. Quite good

5. Which of the following would you prefer to be doing?

    a. Walking the dog
    b. Pottering about in the garden
    c. Painting and decorating

6. Which do you think you have most of, the Wisdom of Solomon or the Patience of Job?

    a. Both, or lack of both, equally
    b. The Wisdom of Solomon
    c. The Patience of Job

7. Which is your least favourite part of a visit to the supermarket?

    a. Going up and down the seemingly endless number of aisles
    b. Queuing at the checkout
    c. I don't really have a least or favourite part of a visit to the supermarket

8. How many books do you read in an average year?

    a. More than one but less than five
    b. One or less
    c. Five or more

9. Do you think people would be justified if they said you did not suffer fools gladly?

    a. Perhaps so, on occasions
    b. Yes, most definitely
    c. No, I believe that would be a very unfair comment

10. You are passed over for promotion at work, unjustly you feel, but your boss tells you that immediately an opportunity arises you will be seriously considered for the next promotion. Would you be prepared to wait for the next opportunity, or start looking for another job with better prospects?

    a. Probably carry on but with less commitment to the job
    b. No, I would start looking for another job immediately
    c. I would carry on and hope my boss was true to his or her word

11. What annoys you most?

    a. Musak being played in your ear while waiting on the telephone to speak to someone
    b. Children shouting and screaming in public places
    c. Bad language in public places

12. Are you a good listener?

    a. Only if I find what I am listening to very interesting
    b. Generally no
    c. Generally yes

13. If you had a pet do you think it would be well trained?

    a. I would probably just train it in the basics as a matter of my duty as a dog owner
    b. Not unless someone else trained it
    c. Yes, I would really enjoy training it

14. You go to buy tickets for a theatrical or sporting event that you would really like to see, but find there is a two-hour queue for tickets. Which of the following is most likely to be your reaction?

    a. In very exceptional circumstances I might queue for two hours
    b. I would not queue and would miss the event as a result
    c. It wouldn't be a problem; I would queue for the two hours to get the tickets

15. Would you ever do a job that involved performing repetitive tasks all day long?

    a. Only if I needed a job, and the money, very desperately
    b. No, I could not possibly do such a job under any circumstances
    c. Yes, I could cope with such a job

16. How often do you lose your temper?

    a. Just occasionally
    b. More than occasionally
    c. Rarely or never

17. What worries you most about having to do jury duty?

    a. The time I would have to spend on it
    b. That I would be able to maintain my concentration throughout a long and complicated hearing
    c. That I will make the correct decision

18. Do you find it difficult to maintain your concentration when attending a lecture or training session?

    a. Only when it is about something in which I am not particularly interested
    b. Yes, I get bored and fidgety and my mind wanders onto other things
    c. No

19. Have you ever complained to someone that they are being too noisy?

    a. No, but I have been on the verge of complaining several times
    b. Yes
    c. No

20. Which of the following words best describes how you think people see you?

    a. changeable
    b. restless
    c. steady

21. Do you think you would make a good driving instructor?

    a. Don't know
    b. No
    c. Yes

22. What is your attitude when you fail an examination?

    a. Disappointed, but may try again later
    b. Will probably move on and try something new
    c. Try harder next time

23. Are you an amber gambler?

    a.   Sometimes

    b.   Yes

    c.   Not generally, as I believe that amber means stop

24. Do you think you could ever write a novel?

    a.   Yes, but I'm not sure I would have the ability

    b.   No

    c.   Yes, it is something I would really like to do, if I ever get the time

25. What do you think about people who queue all night for the New Year Sales or to watch their favourite player at Wimbledon?

    a.   If that's what they want to do it's fine by me, but I cannot ever see me doing it

    b.   They amaze me as it is something I could never do

    c.   Good luck to them if that's what they want to do, and I wouldn't rule out the possibility of doing it myself sometime

Assessment

Award yourself 2 points for every 'c' answer, 1 point for every 'a' and 0 points for every 'b'.

40–50 points

You are in the fortunate position of possessing oodles of patience. Patience is more than just a virtue. To possess it is one of life's great bonuses. It enables us to complete tasks, to tolerate the shortcomings of others and to be able to wait for the right opportunity to come along. It enables us to reach greater academic heights, because we have the patience to study, concentrate and revise, and in our personal life it enables us to work at, and persevere with, relationships.

Just as long as you remember that everything does not necessarily come to those who wait, and that sometimes it is necessary to make things happen, you have a temperament that must be the envy of many of us who are not so fortunate to possess these qualities.

25–39 points

You are likely to possess a great deal of patience when it comes to certain things, but not others. If you like doing a certain thing then you have patience in abundance. However, if the task is not something you enthuse about, then even if that task is a necessary one you may find difficulty getting round to doing it, or completing it once you have started. It is necessary, therefore, to try to discipline yourself to complete such tasks, and for this purpose you might find it useful to make lists and realistic timetables and then strive to adhere to them.

It may be that you have a great deal of patience when it comes to completing practical tasks but not in dealing with people, or vice versa. Because there are so many different types of patience, a certain degree of self-analysis may prove useful, as before we can try to strengthen our weaknesses we must in the first instance be capable of recognizing them.

Less than 25 points

It does not appear that you possess a great deal of patience for many things, and unfortunately this is the way many of us are; it is simply part of our character. One positive aspect of having this type of character is that you may be quite a dynamic person who makes a great deal happen in their life, and if something does not happen quickly you move on to try something else that you hope will achieve a quicker result. However, the negative aspects of impatience do considerably outweigh the positive aspects.

It may be useful for you to analyse your responses to each of the questions in this test and consider carefully, in particular, those responses where you have scored 0 points. It may be that you lack patience for only certain things or situations, and this is something that you need to work hard on.

You should find that this is well worth the effort, as having patience is, indeed, a virtue from which we can reap many rewards, not least that we will feel less stress in our lives, and less overwhelmed with many of the tasks we need to undertake. As a result, our general attitude, well-being and quality of life will be considerably improved.

15

Would you make a good contestant on Big Brother?

In recent years, there has been a rapid increase in fly-on-the-wall documentary series and quiz shows, for instance *The Villa* and *Survival*. However, by far the most famous and popular of these is *Big Brother*, which has become almost a national institution in several countries throughout the world.

In *Big Brother*, up to 12 contestants are locked in a house together for several weeks, remote from newspapers and television and contact with their friends and families, and with very basic living facilities. Their every intimate movement is observed 24 hours a day by cameras placed strategically around the house, and they are given various tasks to perform by the programme's producers, the success or failure of which will determine their food budget for the following week.

In various series, contestants have been filmed arguing, apparently falling in and out of love, fighting, frolicking naked in hot tubs, making love, forming cliques and friendships, showering and undergoing every emotion from wild elation to deep despair.

Each week each contestant must nominate two housemates they would like to see evicted from the house, and give their reasons for doing so. The housemates with the highest number of nominations are then 'up for eviction', which is put to a public vote, with the housemate receiving the most public votes having to leave the house.

The *Big Brother* series is a psychologist's delight. The housemates come from widely differing backgrounds and because, inevitably, their personalities are different, it is part of the programme's attraction to be able to observe how these personalities, whether they be cool and confident, down-to-earth, young, vulnerable and hypersensitive, charismatic or obsessive, will develop, how the contestants will react to the different situations they will face and how they will interact with each other. In the summer of 2002's UK *Big Brother*, for example, the programme's producers were successfully able to spice up the programme, to the delight of the viewers and the media, which resulted in higher tensions between the contestants and record viewing figures.

Even if you are not already a convert to the programme the following test should give you some idea as to whether you could possibly make a successful *Big Brother* contestant. In each of the following, choose from a scale of 1–5 which of these statements you most agree with or is most applicable to you. Choose just one of the numbers 1–5 in each of the 25 statements. Choose 5 for most agree/most applicable, down to 1 for least agree/least applicable.

1. I am very outgoing and extrovert

    5   4   3   2   1

2. I would go on *Big Brother* for the life-enriching experience rather than to try to win the money

    5   4   3   2   1

3. The thought of being isolated from the rest of the world for up to six weeks does not worry me

    5   4   3   2   1

4. The thought of being seen nude on national television and in front of a worldwide internet audience does not concern me

    5   4   3   2   1

5. I believe that appearing on *Big Brother* could make me a stronger person both physically and mentally and lead to bigger and better things in my life

    5   4   3   2   1

6. It is possible that I may form close relationships with some of the other contestants

    5   4   3   2   1

7. I am in good enough shape physically to perform any of the strenuous tasks that *Big Brother* may set me

    5   4   3   2   1

8. I am strong enough mentally to endure six weeks in the *Big Brother* house

    5   4   3   2   1

9. I would stay the course for the whole six weeks if necessary, and would not 'want out' after a couple of weeks

    5   4   3   2   1

10. I would find the task of voting people off one of the most difficult

    5   4   3   2   1

11. I would have no problem accepting the discipline, rules and regulations of the *Big Brother* house

    5   4   3   2   1

12. I am a leader rather than a follower

    5   4   3   2   1

13. I make friends easily and quickly

    5   4   3   2   1

14. I am adaptable and can turn my hands to most things

    5   4   3   2   1

15. I have a good and broad sense of humour

    5   4   3   2   1

16. Even though I may miss my friends and family, it is a situation that I could cope with

    5   4   3   2   1

17. I am not embarrassed when sexual innuendoes start flying

    5   4   3   2   1

18. It would not worry me what the national press were saying about me while I was in the *Big Brother* house

    5   4   3   2   1

19. I never bear grudges

    5   4   3   2   1

20. I am not oversensitive

     5   4   3   2   1

21. I would welcome the experience of sleeping in a dormitory with a group of people I have only just met

     5   4   3   2   1

22. I would welcome the experience of a back-to-basics communal existence for up to six weeks without modern home comforts such as my own room, television and radio

     5   4   3   2   1

23. I would not anticipate a problem adjusting back to normal living after my *Big Brother* experience is ended

     5   4   3   2   1

24. I can accept that during my time in the *Big Brother* house I would have little or no privacy

     5   4   3   2   1

25. I would be able to contribute fully to all the household tasks necessary in the *Big Brother* house, such as cooking, budgeting, cleaning etc

     5   4   3   2   1

Assessment

Total score 90–125

It appears you have the necessary credentials to become a *Big Brother* contestant. You are obviously an extrovert who does not mind being the centre of attention and baring your soul, and everything else, to the nation.

If you did apply, and were successful, the rewards can be great, providing you are able to accept that your life will become the centre of media attention and bad things will be written about you as well as good. Many *Big Brother* contestants have moved onto bigger and better things in their lives as a result of their appearance on the programme and have come out of their experience much stronger mentally than they were before the experience.

Total score 65–89

It is doubtful that you could go through the *Big Brother* experience unscathed and emerge a stronger person as a result. If you did take the plunge then you could only be a successful contestant by being yourself. The spotlight on each of the contestants is intense. If they try to be someone different from what they are, then this will soon be spotted. Likewise, if they try to employ any underhand tactics they will soon be found out.

Contestants can only survive providing they are true to their own character. Then the other contestants, and more importantly the viewing public, will accept them for what they are. They will either like what they see, in which case they are in with a chance of becoming the outright winner, or dislike what they see, in which case they will soon be evicted. In many ways, the *Big Brother* series mirrors life itself, if at times in a somewhat exaggerated way.

Total score less than 65

You will most certainly not make a successful *Big Brother* contestant. Don't even think about it!!

16

Are you a career person?

1. Have you ever gone out of your way to make friends with those you consider to be *the right people*?

   a. No
   b. Yes, it is important to know the right people if you want to get ahead in life
   c. Sometimes, as it does help on occasions to know the right people

2. How frustrating is it for you to be passed over for promotion?

   a. Not at all frustrating
   b. More than frustrating – it hurts!
   c. A little frustrating perhaps but I soon get over it

3. How hard do you push yourself at work?

   a. No harder than I have too – life's too short
   b. Very hard in order to achieve my ambitions
   c. Perhaps a little harder than I should

4. Which of the following would give you most satisfaction?

    a. To be secure and happy in my chosen profession

    b. To be highly successful and get to the top in my chosen career

    c. To be highly regarded and respected as someone who is extremely good at their job

5. How important to you are success and recognition?

    a. I would find success and recognition more satisfying than important

    b. Very important

    c. Quite important

6. Your company is opening a new office in a different part of the country and offers you the job of branch manager. Which of the following is likely to be your reaction, assuming you are settled and happy in your existing home?

    a. I would be very reluctant to move

    b. I would wish to move and expect that my family would be pleased for me and support me in my decision

    c. I would talk it over with my family and reach a joint decision with them

7. Would you ever tell an untruth in order to gain promotion?

    a. No

    b. Yes

    c. Maybe

8. How easy is it for you to switch off from work at weekends and holidays?

    a. Very easy

    b. I never completely switch off from work at weekends and holidays

    c. Sometimes it is difficult to switch off completely

9. How often do you bring work home at night in order to meet a deadline?

    a. Rarely or never
    b. More than occasionally
    c. Occasionally

10. How important is it to you that people in influential positions are aware of your qualifications and achievements?

    a. Not very important
    b. Extremely important
    c. Fairly important

11. Do you always like to know everything that is going on at your place of work?

    a. No
    b. Yes
    c. Not everything, but I like to take an interest in the company in general

12. Do you believe that you should be at the top of your chosen career?

    a. No, I will gladly leave that sort of pressure to others
    b. Yes
    c. If not at the top, perhaps higher up the ladder than I am now

13. Do you feel you are an expert in your chosen field?

    a. No
    b. Yes
    c. There is much more I need to learn

14. Do you talk a great deal about your job to your friends and family?

    a.   No, I believe in switching off and not boring people about what I do for a living

    b.   Yes, I probably do

    c.   I am not aware that I do

15. What do you believe is the main purpose of obtaining qualifications?

    a.   It stretches and exercises the mind and makes you feel you have achieved something

    b.   To obtain a good job and further one's career

    c.   To have a good CV

16. Would you spend six months working abroad away from your family and friends if you had the opportunity?

    a.   Very unlikely

    b.   Yes

    c.   Probably

17. How important is it for you to keep on the right side of the right people?

    a.   Not particularly important

    b.   Very important

    c.   I try to keep on the right side of everyone

18. Which of the following is the most important to you?

    a.   To earn an honest living

    b.   To be in a position of status

    c.   To be respected by my work colleagues

19. Are you looking forward to the day when you can retire and live a life of leisure?

   a. Yes indeed!
   b. Not at all, I would probably never retire if I had the choice
   c. It is not something I am eagerly looking forward to, but I hope to make the most of my retirement when it arrives

20. If you wake up one morning feeling particularly groggy and suspect you may be coming down with a dose of flu, which of the following would you be most likely to do?

   a. I would probably telephone in sick and return to work when I was fit to do so
   b. Go to work and soldier on for as long as I could
   c. It would be foolish to go to work in that condition, so I would probably take the day off and hope I would be fit for work the following day

21. How much time and thought do you give to the way you dress and present yourself for work?

   a. It is not something I give a great deal of thought to
   b. Quite a bit, as my image at work is very important to me
   c. As much as it needs to look as smart and presentable as the next person

22. When attending a job interview, which of the following do you believe is the most important?

   a. To come over as someone who is intelligent and enthusiastic
   b. To look good and have a quiet air of confidence
   c. To be highly qualified and have a good CV

23. If you were made redundant suddenly and unexpectedly, which of the following is most likely to be your immediate reaction?

    a.   How on earth am I going to break the news to my family?

    b.   Totally devastated that I will have to find another job and possibly start again on the bottom rung of the ladder

    c.   A feeling of shock and rejection

24. Which do you enjoy most, your job or your hobbies?

    a.   My hobbies

    b.   My job

    c.   Both the same

25. Do you believe it is necessary to be crafty in order to climb the ladder of success?

    a.   If it is necessary, then it is not for me, as it is not in my nature to be crafty

    b.   Most definitely

    c.   It may help on occasions

26. Would you cancel a holiday in order to meet an important deadline at work?

    a.   Apart from perhaps doing it to save my job I cannot think of any circumstances when I would

    b.   Yes, I would under certain circumstances consider it my duty to do so

    c.   I would be very reluctant indeed to do so

27. Would you put your social life on hold in order to further your career prospects?

    a.   No

    b.   Yes

    c.   Perhaps some but not all

28. Would you pay for an expensive and time-consuming training course if you thought it would further your career?

    a. Very unlikely
    b. Yes
    c. Perhaps

29. Would you take a pay cut if you thought that in the long run it would further your career?

    a. I would never take a pay cut on the chance it would further my career
    b. Yes, if I thought it would benefit me in the long term
    c. Very unlikely

30. Could you be a 'yes person' to someone you despised, if you thought it would further your career?

    a. No way!
    b. Yes
    c. Maybe, but it would be a very bitter pill to swallow

Assessment

Award yourself 2 points for every 'b' answer, 1 point for every 'c' and 0 points for every 'a'.

45–60 points

Your score indicates that you are very much a career person, and that possibly your career is the most important thing in your life. You will do everything in your power to ensure that you are successful in your chosen career. You see your career not just as your way of life, but as a gateway to creating wealth, and possibly prominence, for you and your family.

The difficulty of being so preoccupied with your own career is keeping a sense of priority in your life. Because of the amount of time and energy that is necessary to create a successful career, the danger is that the career person will become a total workaholic to the single-minded exclusion of everything else.

27–44 points

You are a career person, but not obsessively so. Whilst your career is important to you it is not so important as your family values, and you believe that having close family ties brings with it the rewards of stability, happiness and long-term purpose in life, and this is what motivates you, more than your career. You are also likely to cultivate other interests and use your leisure time effectively.

You are likely to be someone who takes pride in their job, and is quietly ambitious, so that if the opportunity presents itself for career advancement you will grasp it, but you are not continually and consciously seeking to advance your career, and career advancement is well down the scale of life's priorities. For many people, being able to strike the right balance between the core values of career, family and contentment means that they are able to reach most of the goals they have set out to achieve in both their personal and private life.

Less than 27 points

Whilst your score indicates that you are not a career person, this does not mean that you are not, or will not be, successful in your chosen career. With many people their career is their source of identity, in other words it is who they are. With you, this is not the case, and your job is merely a part of who you are, along with many other things.

What we are in life is often the result of what values motivate us. What may motivate you is happiness and fulfilment rather than career success. Whilst many people see happiness and fulfilment in being a high-flyer, for you it may be a stable family life, a steady job with not too much responsibility and a regular income. None of us can really find happiness in becoming what we really do not want to be.

17

How obsessive are you?

1. Do you ever worry over whether some small duty or task has been performed?
   a. Very rarely
   b. Occasionally
   c. More than occasionally

2. How important is it for you to keep up with the latest trends and fashions?
   a. Not at all important, it is something I think about very little
   b. Not very important, but it is something I like to be aware of
   c. Very important

3. How often do you clean your car?
   a. Less than six times a year
   b. Between six and 12 times a year
   c. More than 12 times a year

4. Which of the following words do you feel is most applicable to you most of the time?

    a. Attentive
    b. Busy
    c. Preoccupied

5. Have you ever had a hobby that has interfered with your job?

    a. No
    b. No, as one of my hobbies is my job
    c. Yes

6. Would you ever stay away from people who were sick, in case you might catch what they have?

    a. No, not unless I was prevented from going near them by someone medically qualified
    b. Perhaps, if they had something contagious
    c. Yes

7. Do you clean your house every time you know you are going to have a visitor?

    a. Not particularly
    b. Only if I know the house needs cleaning and it is a special visitor
    c. Yes, I tend to make sure the house is looking its best whoever is coming

8. Do you find yourself frequently falling in and out of love?

    a. No
    b. Sometimes but not frequently
    c. Yes

9. Are you subject to frequent mood swings?

    a.   No

    b.   Sometimes but not frequently

    c.   Yes

10. How soon do you start packing for a holiday?

    a.   Usually at the very last minute

    b.   Probably two or three days before

    c.   Up to a week before

11. How often do you look at your watch on average?

    a.   Less than five times a day

    b.   Between five and 10 times a day

    c.   More than 10 times a day

12. Do you set the burglar alarm every time you leave the house and before you go to bed at night?

    a.   I do not have a burglar alarm

    b.   I usually set it every time I leave the house, but not when I go to bed at night

    c.   Yes

13. Do you take care to eat only what you think is good for you?

    a.   No, I generally eat what I enjoy

    b.   Sometimes I will not eat something if I feel it has disagreed with me in the past

    c.   Yes, I do take care with what I eat

14. Do you worry about your appearance?

    a.   Not at all, people will have to take me as they find me

    b.   Not worry, but I like to take some degree of pride in my appearance

    c.   Yes I do tend to worry about what others might think of my appearance

15. Has your hobby ever interfered with a relationship?

    a.   No

    b.   No, as I tend to share my interests with my nearest and dearest

    c.   Yes

16. How often do you take a gamble in any form, for example, such things as lottery tickets, horse racing or bingo?

    a.   Never or very rarely

    b.   Less than five times a week

    c.   Five times a week or more

17. How many television programmes are you hooked on, to the extent that you never miss a programme?

    a.   Less than three

    b.   Between three and five

    c.   Six or more

18. Have you ever kept newspaper cuttings, or photographs of a famous celebrity?

    a.   No

    b.   Yes, photographs only, or cuttings only

    c.   Yes, both photograph and cuttings

19. Have you ever experienced stress and anxiety because you have missed an exercise workout?

    a.   No, I don't workout on a regular basis

    b.   No, but I do like to workout on a regular basis

    c.   Yes

20. How often do you clean your shoes?

    a.   Only when my partner tells me they need cleaning

    b.   Only when I can see they need cleaning

    c.   Every time I wear them

21. How often do you go on a spending spree for personal items such as clothes?

  a. Only when I am in specific need of something
  b. Just occasionally when I feel the need to treat myself or cheer myself up
  c. Every time I get the opportunity

22. Do you save money on a regular basis?

  a. No
  b. No, but I put something aside for a rainy day when I can
  c. Yes, for peace of mind, security and for a rainy day

23. Does having tasks and jobs that are incomplete worry you?

  a. No
  b. Yes, but only occasionally
  c. Yes, more than occasionally

24. Is there any part of your life that you would desperately like to give up, but find that you cannot?

  a. No
  b. Not at the moment, but I have been in such situations in the past and have overcome them
  c. Yes

25. How often do you find yourself washing your hands even though they may not be dirty?

  a. Very rarely
  b. Only occasionally
  c. More than occasionally

Analysis

In its mildest form an obsession is a preoccupation with some task or duty whereby you cannot rest until that task has been performed. There are many such obsessions, as with, for example, the need to clean and polish your car almost daily, do the washing up immediately after every meal, or set off to work at precisely the same time every day. There are also other obsessions most of us can identify with and that we all experience from time to time. The very act of falling in love, for example, can be said to be a type of obsession.

In psychology the definition of obsession is any idea that constantly invades one's thoughts. Many such obsessions can seem almost beyond one's will and even though we may be aware of them there seems to be very little we can do about them. In its most extreme form, obsession is classed as an anxiety disorder. Such obsessions are repetitive thoughts, images, ideas and impulses that seem to make no sense to the person they are affecting, yet they are to that person a cause of much worry and stress.

Sometimes it is difficult to recognize the symptoms of obsession. An example of this is the obsessive exerciser who may experience some, or all, of the following symptoms:

- each time they exercise they push themselves harder and harder;
- they feel stressed if they miss a workout;
- they would prefer to exercise than to do other things they enjoy;
- they need to force themselves to exercise even if they feel fatigued or unwell;
- they worry that they will be out of condition if they miss a session;
- exercising ceases to become fun;
- they cannot relax if they miss out on a session.

These symptoms are typical of many other forms of obsession, sometimes referred to as obsessive compulsive disorder (OCD).

Assessment

Award yourself 2 points for every 'a' answer, 1 point for every 'b' and 0 points for every 'c'.

36–50 points

Your score indicates that you are no more obsessive than the average person. You are no more prone to worry and stress than the rest of us, and are likely to have a relaxed attitude to life in general.

21–35 points

Although you are not an obsessive person, your score does indicate there may be areas in which you do feel anxiety and there may be some tasks that you feel the need to perform that are not, in reality, as important as you sometimes believe them to be. So, although you have no cause for concern in general, it may be advantageous to analyse your responses to the individual questions in this test, and think about any areas where you have scored 0, to ensure there is no danger of any little obsessions creeping into your life.

Less than 20 points

It does appear that in many ways you can be very obsessive. Obsession does affect us in many ways. Sometimes it is merely obsession with finishing a particular task; in other cases it can be more serious. Mildly obsessive people may find they are obsessed with different things at different times. What they are obsessed with one week may not be the same thing they are obsessed with doing the following week. However, more seriously obsessive people may find that it is just one type of obsession that dominates their lives on a permanent basis, as in the exercise example given in the analysis.

The first step to overcoming any obsession is to recognize that you are obsessed. Because of your score on this test it may, therefore, be beneficial to analyse your answers to the individual questions in the test, in particular, the questions where you have scored 0. It is in these areas that you may need to think about whether you are performing a certain task too much, and why, and whether these repetitive habits really should be so important to you.

18

How laid-back are you?

In each of the following, rank the four statements in each group according to which is most applicable to you, which is least applicable, and which of the remaining two are next most applicable and next least applicable.

1.

a. Noise is not something that bothers me very much at all
b. Noise does sometimes annoy me
c. Noise aggravates me a great deal
d. I can usually put up with noise although I prefer peace and solitude

2.

a. I do not have a job in which I feel pressurized in any way
b. I sometimes feel pressurized at work
c. My job involves a great deal of pressure and working to tight deadlines
d. Although my job is a busy one I get through all my workload in my own good time

3.

a.   I feel that I have a very relaxed attitude to life in general
b.   I sometimes feel that I need to relax more
c.   People frequently tell me that I should relax more
d.   I only feel completely relaxed at weekends and on holiday

4.

a.   I like to do things in my own time and at my own pace
b.   I prefer to live to a set routine
c.   I feel very much ruled by time
d.   I always make sure that I am never late for appointments

5.

a.   I usually try to think before I speak
b.   I talk fairly fast but do not gesticulate
c.   I am a very fast talker and tend to gesticulate a lot
d.   I am not a fast talker but do gesticulate a little

6.

a.   Queues and traffic jams do not particularly bother me
b.   Queues and traffic jams do annoy me
c.   I tend to get quite agitated in queues and traffic jams
d.   I try to avoid queues and traffic jams if possible because my
     time could be better spent

7.

a.   Anyone can make mistakes
b.   I cannot afford to make mistakes
c.   I get very angry with myself if I make a mistake
d.   I always try to analyse my mistakes to ensure I don't repeat
     them in the future

8.

a.   I spend a lot of time relaxing by watching television
b.   I usually don't just sit watching television as I like to be doing other things at the same time
c.   I cannot usually sit down to watch television for long periods because I have too much to do
d.   I like to plan ahead what I watch on television

9.

a.   I try not to criticize other people
b.   I am sometimes critical of others
c.   I am often critical of others
d.   I tend not to criticize other people very much

10.

a.   Life is only a game, and you win some, lose some
b.   I always play to win
c.   It is important to me that I am one of life's winners
d.   Winning is one of life's bonuses

Assessment

Scoring instructions (place a tick in the appropriate column for each letter):

Group	Most	Next most	Next least	Least	Score
1.					
a.	☐	☐	☐	☐	☐
b.	☐	☐	☐	☐	☐
c.	☐	☐	☐	☐	☐
d.	☐	☐	☐	☐	☐

2.
a. ☐ ☐ ☐ ☐ ☐
b. ☐ ☐ ☐ ☐ ☐
c. ☐ ☐ ☐ ☐ ☐
d. ☐ ☐ ☐ ☐ ☐

3.
a. ☐ ☐ ☐ ☐ ☐
b. ☐ ☐ ☐ ☐ ☐
c. ☐ ☐ ☐ ☐ ☐
d. ☐ ☐ ☐ ☐ ☐

4.
a. ☐ ☐ ☐ ☐ ☐
b. ☐ ☐ ☐ ☐ ☐
c. ☐ ☐ ☐ ☐ ☐
d. ☐ ☐ ☐ ☐ ☐

5.
a. ☐ ☐ ☐ ☐ ☐
b. ☐ ☐ ☐ ☐ ☐
c. ☐ ☐ ☐ ☐ ☐
d. ☐ ☐ ☐ ☐ ☐

6.
a. ☐ ☐ ☐ ☐ ☐
b. ☐ ☐ ☐ ☐ ☐
c. ☐ ☐ ☐ ☐ ☐
d. ☐ ☐ ☐ ☐ ☐

7.

a. ☐ ☐ ☐ ☐ ☐
b. ☐ ☐ ☐ ☐ ☐
c. ☐ ☐ ☐ ☐ ☐
d. ☐ ☐ ☐ ☐ ☐

8.

a. ☐ ☐ ☐ ☐ ☐
b. ☐ ☐ ☐ ☐ ☐
c. ☐ ☐ ☐ ☐ ☐
d. ☐ ☐ ☐ ☐ ☐

9.

a. ☐ ☐ ☐ ☐ ☐
b. ☐ ☐ ☐ ☐ ☐
c. ☐ ☐ ☐ ☐ ☐
d. ☐ ☐ ☐ ☐ ☐

10.

a. ☐ ☐ ☐ ☐ ☐
b. ☐ ☐ ☐ ☐ ☐
c. ☐ ☐ ☐ ☐ ☐
d. ☐ ☐ ☐ ☐ ☐

Score 0 points for every 'a' answer ticked in Most, 1 point for every 'a' answer ticked in Next most, 2 points for every 'a' answer ticked in Next least and 3 points for every 'a' answer ticked in Least.

Score 2 points for every 'b' answer ticked in Most, 3 points for every 'b' answer ticked in Next most, 1 point for every 'b' answer ticked in Next least and 0 points for every 'b' answer ticked in Least.

Score 3 points for every 'c' answer ticked in Most, 2 points for every 'c' answer ticked in Next most, 1 point for every 'c' answer ticked in Next least and 0 points for every 'c' answer ticked in Least.

Score 0 points for every 'd' answer ticked in Most, 1 point for every 'd' answer ticked in Next most, 3 points for every 'd' answer ticked in Next least and 2 points for every 'd' answer ticked in Least.

80–120 points

Your score indicates you are often on a very short fuse and quite intolerant of the many things that really annoy you. Because of your temperament you find that many small things annoy you that do not particularly concern most other people. As this is in your nature, and likely to be the way you deal with things, it is easier said than done to relax more and try not to let things concern you so much.

This type of temperament manifests itself in many ways. You are likely to be very competitive, also quite ambitious, always in a hurry, rather impatient and easily irritated if things do not go your way, or things are not to your liking. Although having a short fuse does mean that you have a release valve for your frustrations, it could have the effect of alienating many people from you. It is also worth bearing in mind that anxiety does lead to stress and stress is the cause of many health problems, sometimes serious ones. So, if it is possible, try to discipline yourself to relax more, and try on occasions not just to count to 10 but step back and reflect on your life a little more. This may help you to get things into proportion so that when you do encounter those little things that irritate you, and which you often build up out of all proportion, you may do so with a much more relaxed attitude and outlook.

40–79 points

Although you do tend to find yourself stressed out and irritable from time to time, this tends to be more of the exception rather than the rule, and you are able to recognize the warning signs that you are pushing yourself too hard. You are, on these occasions, able to slow down, control your feelings, walk away from problems and push those little irritations to the back of your mind, realizing that in the overall scheme of things they are of very little importance. Even though you may be well-motivated, and possibly quite ambitious, you are not dominated by work and its pressures.

39 points or less

You are in what many would call the fortunate position of having an extremely laid-back and almost totally relaxed attitude to life. You are likely to be regarded by others as someone who is calm, casual, easy-going and patient. This does not necessarily mean that you are not ambitious, but it does mean that you prefer to work away quietly and unspectacularly towards your goal.

Whilst you are in the happy position of being someone who is able to take life as it comes and in your stride, the only word of caution is that sometimes we need to inject a little passion into our lives and make things happen. The danger for some people is that they tend to be so laid-back they almost fall over and are horizontal.

19

Laterality

The meaning of the word lateral is 'of, or relating to, the side, away from the median axis'. In general, the term laterality can refer to any preference for one side of the body over another. Probably the most common example of this, and one to which we can all relate, is whether a person is left-handed or right-handed.

If we were to remove a brain from the skull, we would see that it is made up of two almost identical hemispheres. These two hemispheres are connected by a bridge, or interface, of millions of nerve fibres called the corpus callosum, which allows them to communicate with each other. In order to work to its full potential, each of these hemispheres must be capable of analysing its own input first, only exchanging information with the other half, by means of the interface, when a considerable amount of processing has taken place. Because both hemispheres are capable of working independently, human beings are able to process two streams of information at once. The brain then compares and integrates the information to obtain a broader and more in-depth understanding of the concept under examination.

In the early 1960s, the US psychologist, Roger Sperry, showed by a series of experiments, first using animals whose corpus callosum had been severed, and then on human patients whose corpus callosum had been severed in an attempt to cure epilepsy, that each of the two hemispheres has developed specialized functions and has its own private sensations, perceptions, ideas and thoughts, all separate from the opposite hemisphere. As their experiments continued, Sperry, who won the 1981 Nobel Prize in medicine for his work in this area, and his team, were able to reveal much more about how the two hemispheres were specialized to perform different tasks.

For most people, the left side of the brain is analytical and functions in a sequential and logical fashion, and is the side that controls language, academic studies and rationality. On the other hand, the right side is creative and intuitive and leads, for example, to the birth of ideas for works of art and music.

The following test is designed to discover whether you are basically a right-sided brain person or a left-sided brain person, or whether you are indeed in the fortunate position of having the right balance between the two brain hemispheres, and to identify the strengths and weaknesses of one-hemisphere domination.

1.   Which of the following appeals to you most?
   a.   To be able to do things because I want to do them
   b.   To have a wonderful family life
   c.   To be highly successful in my chosen career

2.   How strongly do you rely on your intuition?
   a.   Very strongly
   b.   Not very strongly although I have occasionally followed my gut feelings
   c.   Hardly ever, as I rely more on reason and logic

3.   Which of these best describes you?
   a.   Inquisitive
   b.   Well organized
   c.   Serious and studious

4. Which of the following most takes your breath away?

    a. One of nature's great wonders such as the Grand Canyon
    b. A great human-made structure such as the Taj Mahal
    c. A great operatic voice such as Pavarotti or Domingo

5. How often do you worry about the way we treat our planet?

    a. Very often
    b. Occasionally
    c. Hardly ever

6. Which of the following do you most admire?

    a. The flight of a bird
    b. The speed and grace of a cheetah
    c. The strength and courage of a lion

7. Do you like to set yourself targets and try to stick to them?

    a. No, I prefer to do things when I feel ready and when I am in the right frame of mind
    b. I do sometimes forward plan but in a flexible sort of way
    c. Yes, as that is the most efficient way to get something done

8. How important to you is punctuality?

    a. Not important
    b. Fairly important
    c. Very important

9. Which of the following do you find most difficult when sitting examinations?

    a. Concentrating and revising
    b. Conquering my nerves beforehand
    c. Worrying about whether I am going to score highly

10. Assuming you had time on your hands, which of the following would most appeal to you?

   a.   Taking up something creative such as painting or sculpture
   b.   Taking up a sport such as golf or bowls
   c.   Joining a health club to keep myself in good shape

11. Which of these words best describes you?

   a.   Complex
   b.   Content
   c.   Calculating

12. How often do you have dreams that you are unable to explain?

   a.   More than occasionally
   b.   Occasionally
   c.   Rarely or never

13. Which of these qualities best sums you up?

   a.   Unconventional
   b.   Wise
   c.   Patient

14. How often do you doodle?

   a.   More than occasionally
   b.   Occasionally
   c.   Less than occasionally

15. Which of the following most irritates you?

   a.   Rules and regulations
   b.   Rudeness
   c.   Incompetence

16. How often do you get flashes of inspiration or new ideas to the extent that your mind cannot rest until you have tried to put them into practice?

 a. More than occasionally
 b. Occasionally
 c. Rarely or never

17. Do you find it difficult to complete a long project or task without breaking off to do other things?

 a. Yes
 b. Occasionally
 c. Not usually

18. What worries you most about retirement?

 a. Nothing worries me about retirement
 b. Perhaps getting older and not being as fit as I was
 c. That I may get bored and have difficulty filling my time

19. Which of the following most closely represents your views on making mistakes?

 a. Making mistakes is all part of life's experience and it is important we learn from them
 b. The only people who do not make mistakes are people who do nothing, and that is the greatest mistake of all
 c. We all make mistakes, but in life the winners make fewer mistakes than life's losers

20. Which of these words best describes you?

 a. Philosophical
 b. Peaceful
 c. Pragmatic

21. What are your views on the phrase: 'so much to do and so little time to do it'?

    a. I agree, and get quite frustrated about it at times

    b. I accept that there are many more things I would like to do if I ever get the opportunity but it is not something that worries or frustrates me

    c. It is not something that I give a great deal of thought to

22. Out of the following three choices, which do you consider was your best subject at school?

    a. Practical subjects such as art or metalwork

    b. Sport

    c. Mathematics

23. Do you believe that aggressive behaviour is sometimes necessary as a means to an end?

    a. Not under any circumstances

    b. Maybe in certain very rare circumstances

    c. Yes

24. How would you best like to be described?

    a. Imaginative and innovative

    b. Amiable and well-liked

    c. Trustworthy and dependable

25. When making an important decision what do you prefer to do?

    a. Make your own decision

    b. Talk things over with someone close and reach a joint decision

    c. Seek advice from an expert

26. How organized are you when it comes to filing away important documents?

    a. Not well organized at all
    b. Reasonably well organized
    c. Extremely well organized

27. Which of the following words do you believe is most applicable to you?

    a. Visionary
    b. Steady
    c. Businesslike

28. Do you channel most of your energies into your chosen career?

    a. No
    b. I do take my career very seriously but have time to enjoy a great many other things besides
    c. Yes, I consider myself a specialist in my chosen career and it takes up a great deal of my time and energy

29. Which of the following best describes you?

    a. Emotional
    b. Decisive
    c. Aggressive

30. Which of the following would most influence your choice of a holiday destination?

    a. Beautiful scenery
    b. Sun, sea and sand
    c. Exciting night life

Analysis

The right and left hemisphere functions can be summarized as follows:

Left hemisphere	*Right hemisphere*
parsing	holistic
logic	intuition
conscious thoughts	subconscious thoughts
outer awareness	inner awareness
methods, rules	creativity
written language	insight
number skills	three-dimensional forms
reasoning	imagination
scientific skills	music, art
aggression	passive
sequential	simultaneous
verbal intelligence	practical intelligence
intellectual	sensuous
analytical	synthetic

The right-hand side of the brain controls the left-hand side of the body and vice versa. While some individuals may be heavily weighted towards a particular hemisphere it does not mean they are predominant in every one of this hemisphere's skills, as no one is entirely left or right-brained. The importance to each one of us in accessing both hemispheres of the brain is considerable. In order to support the whole brain function, logic and intuition, for example, are equally important. Generally, however, education systems in the Western world tend, particularly as we live in a world of specialization, to develop the analytical capacities of the left hemisphere at the expense of the creative talents of the right. Indeed, there was a time, not so long ago, when many schools would make left-handed pupils learn to write with their right hand, but thankfully this is no longer the case today.

Assessment

Award yourself 2 points for every 'a' answer, 1 point for every 'b' and 0 points for every 'c'.

48–60 points

This score indicates that you are a right-sided brain person. It is the right side of our brain that controls spatial ability, artistic expression, creative thought, inner awareness and, therefore, many of our subconscious thoughts and emotional reactions.

The right side is the intuitive hemisphere, which imagines and perceives things holistically. In other words, you like to see the big picture, rather than seeing the component details. As such, it is the side of the brain that reconstructs a whole pattern out of individual pieces, at the same time giving rise to our dreams, ideas and concepts.

It is also likely that as a right-brained person you have an appreciation of art and music. As a predominantly right-sided brain person you tend to learn in a subconscious and creative way, leading to an emotional reaction to situations as opposed to a measured and logical analysis. On many occasions it is possible you have arrived at the correct answer to a question or problem without being sure how the answer was arrived at, and this is where intuition is so important to the right-sided brain person.

As the left side of the brain tends to process things in sequence as opposed to the right-brain approach, which is random, you may find that you have a tendency to move from one task to another before the first task is completed. This can often be a disadvantage as you can find yourself with several different tasks all uncompleted. It may, therefore, assist if you can start making lists and schedules to discipline yourself to complete tasks more efficiently, and by setting yourself deadlines.

30–47 points

You would appear to have a good balance between the left and right hemispheres without being over-dominated by either side. While this is a considerable advantage, it is nevertheless no cause for complacency. One side-effect of hemispherical balance is that you could feel more conflict than someone with clearly established dominance. Occasionally this conflict will be between what you feel and what you think and may involve how you tackle problems and interpret information.

On the positive side, the advantage of having a balanced brain is that with problem solving you can perceive the big picture and the essential details at the same time. An architect, for example, needs to balance creativity with logic and detail in order to turn a concept into a workable reality.

It is of considerable advantage to balanced brain individuals that they have the natural ability to succeed in multiple fields due to the great flexibility of mind that they possess. The learning and thinking process is likely to be enhanced when both sides of the brain work in a balanced manner.

Less than 30 points

Like the vast majority of people in this world you are predominantly a left-sided brain dominated person. The left side of the brain is analytical and functions in a sequential and rational fashion and is the side that controls language, academic studies and rationality. The left-brain person will tend to process information from part to whole, that is, in a linear manner, as opposed to the right-sided brain person who likes to be able to see the big picture first.

The left brain also tends to process things in sequence as opposed to in a random order and is likely to be a fine accountant or planner. Also, spelling is likely to be a strong point of the left-brain person, as spelling involves sequencing.

Left-sided brain people are also much more likely to be specialists in their chosen field.

It may be advantageous to the predominantly left-brain person to employ certain right-brain strategies, in particular, the development of creative thinking skills and intuition. When attending a lecture, for example, a right-brain student may be at a disadvantage unless they have been given an overview of the whole concept first, as they essentially need to know exactly what they are doing and why. On the other hand, the left-brain student may not find it necessary to look this far ahead, but perhaps would find it helpful to do so.

20

Creativity

The term creativity refers to mental processes that lead to solutions, ideas, concepts, artistic expression, theories or products that are unique and novel. Because it is such a diverse subject in which there are so many different ways in which creativity manifests itself, and because in so many people it is to a great extent unexplored, creativity is very difficult to measure.

The French mathematicians, Poincaré and Hadamard, defined the following four stages of creativity:

Preparation: the attempt to solve a problem by normal means

Incubation: when you feel frustrated that the above methods have not worked and, as a result, you then move away to other things

Illumination: the answer suddenly comes to you in a flash via your subconscious

Verification: your reasoning powers take over as you analyse the answer that has come to you, and you assess its feasibility

The creative functions are controlled by the right-hand hemisphere of the human brain. This is the side of the brain that is underused by the majority of people, as opposed to the thought processes of the left-hand hemisphere, which is characterized by order, sequence and logic. Because it is underused, much creative talent remains untapped throughout life. Until we try, most of us never know what we can achieve. For example, one in three people in Britain has a desire to write a novel, yet only a very small percentage of these people progress further than the initial stage of just thinking about it.

We all have a creative side to our brain, therefore we all have the potential to be creative. However, because of the pressures of modern living and the need for specialization, many of us never have the time or opportunity, or indeed are given the encouragement, to explore our latent talents, even though most of us have sufficient ammunition to realize this potential in the form of data that has been fed into, collated and processed by the brain over many years.

Writers, indeed all artists, must use both halves of their brain. They must use the right side of the brain to create things and the left side of the brain to organize things. The creative and intuitive right side is able to cope with complexity and is where insights originate, whilst the left side controls language, academic studies and rational intellectual work. The problem is getting these two halves of the brain to pass information back and forth and work together, especially as, in many people, the left half of the brain is possessively dominant.

In order to perform any creative task it is necessary to encourage your right side to start its creative juices flowing; in other words, move your mental processes, albeit temporarily, from the dominant left side across to the creative right side. This may sound fine in theory, but is not so easy to put into practice.

So, how can the predominantly left-sided brain person encourage the right side of his or her brain to be more creative? Since such a person is so dominated by the left brain, one way is to lull your left brain into a degree of inactivity, or even bore it to sleep. This may, for example, occur on a long train journey or plane trip. At such times, your right brain has the opportunity to become more creative because it has less strong opposition from the fact-cluttered dominant left side. At such times, have a pocket tape recorder or jotter by your side and make a note of all the thoughts that occur to you no matter how strange, irrelevant or random they may seem. Most ideas or insights occur at random just for an instant. If you do not record them, they are gone just as quickly, and are probably lost forever.

At night too, ideas come to us and our mind often behaves in a seemingly strange way. Again, this is because our logical and analytical left side is at its most inactive, and our subconscious right side is to the fore, behaving in a mysterious and irrational way, giving rise to dreams and nightmares, of which we often can make little sense. Many writers keep notepads at their bedsides and force themselves to arouse from their half-sleep to jot these ideas, dreams and creative thoughts down.

In these periods of brain activity do not pause to evaluate such ideas to decide which are of use and which are not. By doing so you will reawaken your dominant left side and will lose many of these thoughts before you have a chance to write them down. The evaluation of ideas is a left brain activity and there will be plenty of time for that later.

So how does one put these newfound ideas into reality and start on the road to producing a first novel? Again, there is the need to relax and put your left brain to sleep. This means no distractions. Most writers closet themselves away in seclusion as this is the only way they are able to create without interruption. Make sure the telephone is turned off, the study door is locked, you are fully relaxed and focused on the job in hand and have no negative thoughts about the task before you.

You are now ready to start. At first, just let the words flow at random for as long as they will. At this stage, there is still not the need for any evaluation. Just keep writing without concerning yourself with spelling or grammar, or whether you are putting down exactly the right word. At this stage the object of the exercise is to get creative ideas on paper and expand on an original creative spark that occurred to you in a period of half-sleep, or boredom during a long plane journey.

Then, when you have written all you can, begin to read it through, then reread it and start adding bits to it and expanding on various parts. Again, ignore your left brain as you are still seeking fresh ideas. At this stage you are rewriting, adding and elaborating, and still generating new creative thoughts.

Finally, it is time for your left brain to be reawakened. There is now the need to organize what you have put down on paper. You accept it's something of a mess. The grammar is awful, so is the spelling, and it does not flow as it should. This is the least of your problems, and is the easiest thing to reorganize. It is what you are good at. Your left brain is now entirely in its element. The main thing is that you have created what you probably never even dreamed was possible. A work completely original to yourself from your own creative thoughts and insight.

Like many other tasks, or pleasures, the majority of us never know what we can achieve until we try. Having then tried, we instinctively know whether we find it enjoyable or whether we have a talent or flair for it. Then, if these signs are positive we must persevere. By cultivating new leisure activities and pursuing new pastimes it is possible for each of us to exploit the potential and often vastly underused parts of the human brain.

The following exercises, while different in themselves, are all designed with the object of improving or recognizing your own powers of mental productivity, generation of ideas and artistic skill.

Exercise 1

In each of the following use your imagination to create an original sketch or drawing of something recognizable incorporating the symbol already provided. You have 30 minutes in which to complete the 12 drawings.

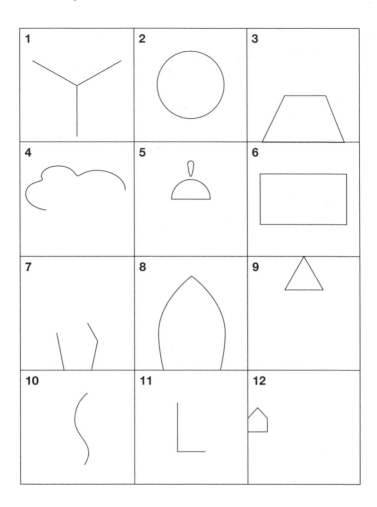

Assessment

You can mark this test yourself. However, it is best marked by a friend or family member. Award one mark for each recognizable sketch, providing it is not similar to any of the other sketches. For example, if you draw a face, a second face scores no point as each sketch must have an original theme. You thus obtain marks for variety. If you are creative you will tend to try to draw something different for each sketch. There is no correct answer to each of the 12 sketches as for each there are any number of ideas.

Scoring
11–12 points   exceedingly creative
7–10   very creative
4–6   average

Repeat the exercise as many times as you wish. Try other geometric objects or lines as a starting point.

Exercise 2

This test is based on Gestalt and Jackson's Test of Divergent Ability, which requires the subject to name as many new uses as possible for everyday objects such as a brick or a piece of string. Here, you are required to name up to 12 new uses for a brick in 10 minutes. You should work strictly to the time limit, otherwise your score will be invalidated.

1....................................   2....................................

3....................................   4....................................

5....................................   6....................................

7....................................   8....................................

9....................................   10...................................

11...................................   12...................................

Assessment

You can mark your efforts yourself, but it is better if you get a friend or family member to do so.

Allow:
2 points for any good or original answer

1 point for a good attempt
0 points for completely impractical answers
0 points for any anti-social answers such as breaking someone's window or hitting someone over the head

Scoring
18–24 points   highly creative
13–17 points   above average
7–12 points   average

Now try the same again but this time think up uses for a 12-inch square piece of cardboard.

1...   2...

3...   4...

5...   6...

7...   8...

9...   10.......................................

11.......................................   12.......................................

Now repeat the exercise as many times as you wish with other common household objects such as a bucket, a comb, a rubber band, a toothbrush or an empty milk bottle.

Exercise 3

The object here is to interpret each of the 12 drawings in the wildest and most imaginative way you can. You may also try playing the game with other people. The main thing is to let your imagination run wild and lose your inhibitions. The more people laugh at your efforts, the more successful you are likely to have been in using your imagination and creativity. For example, you might think that drawing number 1 is a bull's-eye or target, but is there anything else it can be? Let your imagination run riot and see what you can come up with.

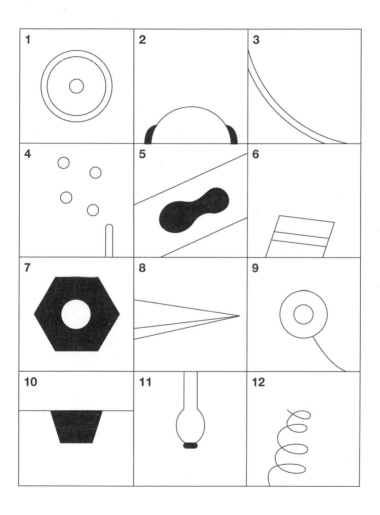

21

Perception

In psychology, the term 'perception' is so broad that it can embrace almost every aspect of the subject. In essence, it encompasses how we perceive ourselves, how we perceive others and how others perceive us. It also envelops how we perceive the world as a whole – the big picture – and how we perceive different events, scenarios and situations that occur within the big picture.

In order to perceive others sympathetically we need to have empathy with them, their character, aspirations and points of view. Similarly, in order to fully understand ourselves we need to recognize and know ourselves for what we are, rather that what we would like to be.

One common cause of incorrect perception is the stereotyping of others. Because sometimes we fall into this trap we tend to prejudge others on what we assume them to be like, even before we get to know them.

One of the most important aspects of perception is the ability to see more than one point of view. The example shown opposite of the Necker cube consists of a simple line drawing.

When you first look at the cube, it appears quite unambiguous and you are quite clear what you are looking at. If, however, you continue to stare at the figure and keep your attention focused on it, the orientation suddenly shifts, then periodically changes back

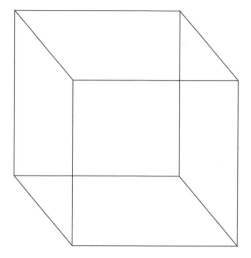

and forth between these two orientations as you continue to focus. In other words, it is a simple figure, yet our perception of it is continually changing.

The Necker cube thus illustrates the importance of perception. Two different viewpoints appear, yet they are both correct. We should, therefore, endeavour to see both viewpoints and, sometimes more specifically, both sides of an argument. This may then enable us to reach a compromise, thus avoiding conflict. At the very least, we should attempt to understand the second viewpoint, even if that point of view is diametrically opposed to our own.

The remainder of this chapter concentrates on just one aspect of perception – *attention*. In order to perceive any situation accurately it must be focused on to the relative exclusion of other distractions. We must, in other words, give it our full and undivided attention and select from all that is occurring around us precisely what we need to focus on at that particular time, and maintain our concentration and state of mental clarity on that situation.

One example of the difficulty in doing this is in a police investigation or court of law where a witness is asked to identify a person or describe an incident. On such occasions, it is commonplace for two genuinely well-intentioned and public-spirited individuals to give opposing versions of an event.

It is also possible to be misled into a false perception, as, for example, in the question: 'How many times does the letter S appear in the name of the world's longest river?' Most people will start to count the number of S letters in the name Mississippi and overlook the fact that the world's longest river is the Nile. The correct answer to the question is, therefore, *none*.

The following test of 12 questions is designed to test your powers of perception and attention to detail, your alertness of mind, in some cases your ability to think laterally, and your ability to avoid falling into the occasional trap that has been set.

In philosophy, perception is defined as 'the complex method of obtaining information about our surrounding world, specifically through our senses and adopting this information as beliefs'. The problem with this is that our perceptions are not always reliable since it is possible for us to misperceive what we believe to be correct and our senses are often susceptible to illusions. It is hoped to demonstrate in a number of the questions that follow that sometimes these fears are well-founded.

Whilst the test is meant to be fun, it should also have the desired effect of strengthening your own powers of perception no matter how well or badly you score. Each answer contains a detailed analysis, not only to highlight the thought processes necessary to tackle each question, but also to explore the reasons why you may not, in some cases, have arrived at the correct solution.

Test of perception

Time limit: 30 minutes

1. How many circles and squares appear below?

2. The time is 19 minutes to the hour. Without looking at a clock, place the following in order reading anticlockwise from the minute hand.

   II   XI   IX   III

3. Emphatically, famous frauds are the cause of many hours of frenzied yet fruitful scientific police research, combined with the experience of years.

   Count the number of times the letter F appears in the sentence above. You must count them just once and not recheck your answer.

4. Why are the words below in the order they are?

   idea, knob, epic, hard, rare, wolf, sing, inch

5. Frank's mother had three children. The first was named June, the second was named May. What was the third child's name?

6. Imagine you are a bus driver. At the first stop, three females, four males and six children get on. At the second stop four children and two females get on and one male gets off. At the third stop one female gets on. How tall is the bus driver?

7. A famous Chinese conjuror claims that without bouncing a ping-pong ball off any surface or object and without tying anything to it, he can hit it with his hand, propelling it a short distance, whereupon it will of its own accord come to a complete stop, and then come back straight to him. How does he perform this feat?

8. Alice sent the following cryptic message to the Cheshire Cat. Can you decode it?

    nia gareh tego tyt pmu htu pt'nd luocn ems'g nikeh tllad nases rohs'g ni kehtl la

9. Apart from triangles and rectangles (four-sided geometric figures) do any other geometric figures appear below?

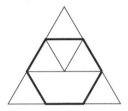

10. What is the connection between these pairs of words?

    NOMAD RIDE

    MELON DONE

    PROM ECHO

    CHOP ARISING

11. You cut a thick piece of wood into 12 equal pieces and stack them in two piles, each pile consisting of six pieces. You then find you have three piles of wood. Why?

12. Under any circumstances is it ever legally possible for a man to marry his widow's daughter?

Answers and answer analysis

1. No circles and no squares.

    Award yourself 4 points for a correct answer.

    Many people will look at the figure and assume that there are four black circles with their corners hidden by a white square. This is, in fact, an illusion created in the imagination of the beholder. All that actually appears are four three-quarter circles positioned in such a way as to give the illusion of a square. If you look closely there is no square and there are no circles.

2. III   II   XI   IX

    Award yourself 2 points for a correct answer.

    There is no trick here. People who get this wrong have usually read the question incorrectly, for example 19 minutes *past* instead of 19 minutes *to* the hour, and reading *clockwise* instead of *anti-clockwise*. There is also a tendency to confuse the similar numerals II and III, and XI and IX.

3. Nine times.

    Award yourself 2 points for a correct answer.

    Surprisingly, on average, people only find six out of the nine on first reading. Many people tend to overlook the F in the word *of* as the brain sees it as V and not F.

4. The last letters of the words are ABCDEFGH

    Award yourself 2 points for a correct answer.

    The requirement here is perception and alertness of mind to look at the end of each word as well as the beginning, or the word as a whole. Whilst the answer is there for all to see, to arrive quickly at this answer we must have the flexibility of mind to explore and analyse all possibilities.

5. Frank.

    Award yourself 3 points for a correct answer.

    There are a number of distractions here that are deliberately designed to lead people into a false perception, even though we are told the answer in the first word of the question. First, we are presented with a seemingly logical sequence – June, May and then, presumably, April. We are also given the names of two girls and, therefore, automatically start to think that the third child is probably also a girl. By the time our mind has been cluttered up with these false perceptions, many will have forgotten that we are told in the opening statement that it is Frank's mother's children we are considering, and as two of her three children are named June and May, the name of her third and remaining child must be Frank himself.

6. As you are the bus driver, then the bus driver is as tall as you are.

    Award yourself 3 points for a correct answer.

    The film director, Alfred Hitchcock, used a technique in many of his movies that he called a 'McGuffin', that is, a storyline that turns out to be totally irrelevant to the remainder of the plot. Such a McGuffin was used in the film *Psycho*, where in the early part of the movie Marion Crane is shown stealing money from her employer and making off with it. She then checks into the Bates Motel, is murdered, and the stolen money is never referred to again. It becomes a forgotten and irrelevant part of the plot, once it has served its purpose in getting Marion Crane to the Bates Motel.

    This puzzle contains such a McGuffin. In the first sentence we are told that you, the reader, are the bus driver. In the final sentence you are asked the height of the bus driver, that is, you. The rest of the question is a complete irrelevance and merely there as a distraction in order to create a false perception of the question.

7.   He hits the ball straight up in the air with his hand.

Award yourself 2 points for a correct answer.

Again, there are McGuffins. The fact that he is a conjuror is irrelevant, as is the fact that he is Chinese. These facts are merely a distraction. It is necessary to pick the bones out of the question, which is to consider simply how it is possible to propel the ball so that it will travel but a short distance, come to a complete stop and then return to the sender.

8.   Read the message backwards, altering word boundaries to uncover the message:

All the King's horses and all the King's men couldn't put Humpty together again.

Award yourself 4 points for a correct answer.

As with most of these puzzles the answer is there in front of you. However, as in the case of question 4, to arrive at this answer we must have sufficient flexibility of mind to quickly explore all possibilities. The tendency is to start analysing each set of letters individually. We tend to build artificial barriers in our minds between the groups of letters. However, the answer you are seeking must break down these barriers, as this then enables us to consider the message as a whole.

9.

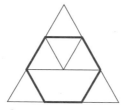

Award yourself 3 points for a correct answer.

The question leads us to assume, correctly, that at least one other geometric figure does appear. The problem is that this figure is not so easy to spot because it is disguised by having other figures within it, whereas the triangles and rectangle are not hidden in this way and stand out clearly for all to see.

10. The connection is capital cities of the world:

NO*MAD RID*E – Madrid
ME*LON DON*E – London
P*ROM E*CHO – Rome
CHO*P ARIS*ING – Paris

Award yourself 3 points for a correct answer.

Once again the answer is there for us to perceive. We are told in the question that we are looking for a *connection between* the *pairs* of words, and the answer is just such a connection. The problem is that many people tend to consider the words as a whole and not look for connecting parts of words. Again, it is necessary to break down the artificial barriers that the mind creates in order to find a solution.

11. The third pile is the sawdust from cutting up the wood.

Award yourself 4 points for a correct answer.

In this instance it is necessary to employ a degree of lateral thinking in order to perceive more than just what the question tells us. The facts appear quite simple, 12 equal pieces (the fact that they are equal is another McGuffin) and two resultant piles of six pieces each. So, our first instinct is that the third pile of wood must have come from some outside source. It is only when we perceive in our mind the act of cutting up so many pieces from one thick piece that we realize that the third pile of wood must, in fact, be a pile of sawdust.

12. No, if he had a widow he would be dead, so could not marry anyone.

Award yourself 3 points for a correct answer.

Again, there is a McGuffin. It is irrelevant to ask if it is legally possible, but this irrelevance has the desired effect with many people of providing a false perception of the problem and shifting the focus of perspective away from the trap. The only thing that is relevant in this case is that if the man has a widow, then he must be dead.

Rating
30–35	exceptionally perceptive
25–29	very perceptive
20–28	above average perception
13–19	average perception
12 or less	below average perception

Section 2

Aptitude Tests

22

How to do the aptitude tests

This section consists of two separate intelligence (IQ) tests designed to measure your verbal and numerical ability, reasoning skills and diagrammatical or spatial reasoning under strictly timed conditions.

In psychology, intelligence is defined as 'the capacity to acquire knowledge or understanding, and to use it in novel situations'. Intelligence is the capacity to learn or understand. Although all people possess intelligence, it varies in amount for each person, and remains the same throughout life from approximately 18 years of age. IQ, or intelligence quotient, is an age-related measure of intelligence and is defined as 100 times mental age. The word quotient means the result of dividing one quantity by another, and intelligence can be defined as mental ability and quickness of mind.

The earliest known attempts to rank people in terms of intelligence date back to the Chinese Mandarin system, c. 500 BC, when studying the works of Confucius enabled successful candidates to enter the public service. The top 1 per cent of candidates were successful in progressing to the next stage, where they would again be run off against each other, and the procedure repeated yet again through a final layer of selection. Thus, the chosen candidates were in the top 1 per cent of the top 1 per cent of the top 1 per cent.

The French psychologists, Alfred Binet and Theodore Simon, devised the first modern intelligence test in 1905. The pair developed a 30-item test with the purpose of ensuring that no child be denied admittance to the Paris school system without formal examination. In 1916, the American psychologist, Lewis Terman, revised the Binet-Simon scale to provide comparison standards for Americans from age three to adulthood. Terman devised the term 'intelligence quotient' and developed the so-called Stanford-Binet intelligence test to measure IQ after joining the Faculty at Stanford University as Professor of Education. The Stanford-Binet test was further revised in 1937 and 1960 and remains today one of the most widely used of all intelligence tests.

An IQ test is, by definition, any test that purports to measure intelligence. Generally, such tests consist of a series of tasks, each of which has been standardized with a large representative population of individuals. Such procedure establishes the average IQ as 100. When measuring the IQ of a child, that child is given an intelligence test that has already been given to thousands of other children, and an average score has been established for each age group. Thus, a child who at eight years of age obtained a result expected of a 10-year-old would score an IQ of 125, that figure being mental age divided by chronological age × 100, or 10/8 × 100. On the other hand, a child of 10 years of age who obtained a result expected of an eight-year-old would score an IQ of 80, or 8/10 × 100. Because mental age remains constant from the age of 18, this method of calculation does not apply to adults. Adults have, instead, to be judged on a standardized IQ test whose average score is 100, and the results graded above and below this score according to known scores.

With aptitude tests in particular it is advantageous to familiarize yourself with the types of questions and recurring themes that you are likely to encounter and the tests that follow will provide valuable practice for readers who may have to take an IQ test in the future.

Because the tests have been specially compiled for this book they have not been standardized; therefore, an actual IQ rating cannot be provided. We do, however, provide a guide to assessing your performance on each of the separate tests.

On all of the tests, you have limited time, and this time limit should be strictly adhered to, otherwise your score will be invalidated. It is, therefore, important that you do not spend too much time on any one question; if in doubt leave it and return to it using the time remaining. If you do not know an answer, it may be well worthwhile having an intuitive guess, as this may well prove to be correct.

23

IQ test one

Introduction

Test one consists of four sub-tests, each of 10 questions, in four different disciplines: spatial ability, logical thought processes, verbal ability and numerical ability. A performance rating is provided for each test of 10 questions to enable you to identify your own strengths or weaknesses and there is also an overall rating for each complete test of 40 questions. It is this overall rating that is the best guide to your performance. You should keep strictly within your time limit, otherwise your score will be invalidated. The answers are at the end of all four tests.

10-question test (time limit 30 minutes)

10	exceptional
8–9	excellent
7	very good
5–6	good
4	average

40-question test (time limit two hours)
36–40   exceptional
31–35   excellent
25–30   very good
19–24   good
14–18   average

Spatial ability test

Read the instructions to each question and study each set of diagrams carefully.

1.

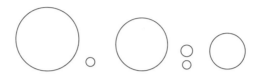

Which set of circles comes next?

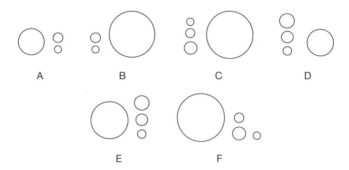

3.   Which is the odd one out?

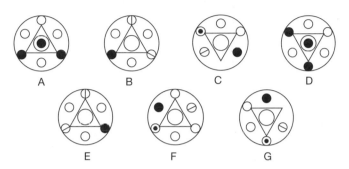

4.

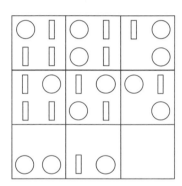

Which is the missing tile?

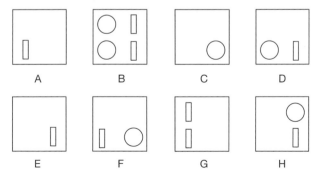

5.

 is to

as

is to

 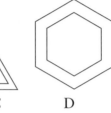 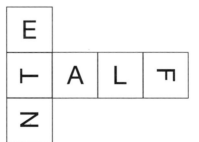 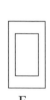

A   B   C   D   E

6.

E
ㅏ A L ㄱ
N

When the above is folded to form a cube, which one of the following can be produced?

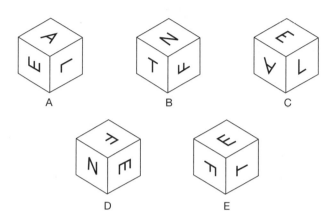

7.

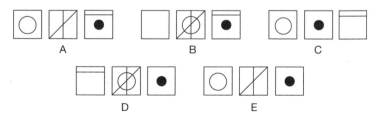

What comes next?

8.

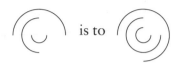 is to

as

is to

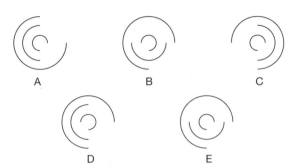

A   B   C

D   E

9.

What comes next?

A   B   C

D   E

10.

Which shield should replace the question mark?

A   B   C   D   E

Logic test

Calculators are not allowed, and are not considered necessary for this test.

1.   What comes next?

CANASTA

ACTRESS

SAUSAGE

ESCAPED

Is it: pagodas, develop, angular, doublet, cabaret?

2.   What number should replace the question mark?

	1				2	1
	3		3	5		
3	4		5	5	4	
3		2		?		2
2				4		
3		3	3	4		2
2	3		3		2	

3.   What letter should replace the question mark?

A   B   C   E   G   J
M   Q   U   Z   E   ?

4.   What number should replace the question mark?
76492, 28467, 76472, 26467, ?

5. Into which of the remaining two squares would you place the letters H and I?

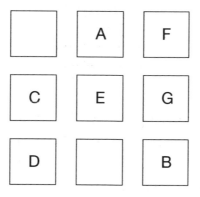

6. Carol beats Peter at golf but loses to Colin. Jill usually wins against Peter, occasionally against Carol but never against Colin. List the four players in order of ability.

7. Which is the odd one out?

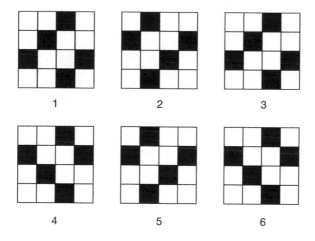

8.   What number should replace the question mark?

3	13	8	7	9
4	7	2	5	6
9	5	6	11	1
10	17	14	16	9
2	6	2	3	?

9.   Which group of letters is the odd one out?

EDKJ   NMTS   IHON   TSYX   POVU

10. What number comes next?

3846721

4672183

7218364

?

Verbal ability test

1. Change one letter only in each of the words below to produce a familiar phrase.

    TAME FOOD CART ON

2. Which two words are most opposite in meaning?

    commendable, plausible, banal, unlikely, receptive, offensive

3. Inside is to magma as outside is to: sulphur, lava, crust, plate, earth, erupt

4. GLACIATED MAT is an anagram of which two words, four letters and eight letters long, which are opposite in meaning?

5. Which word in brackets is most similar in meaning to the word in capitals?

    PENITENT (pervasive, apologetic, impecunious, callous, invasive)

6. Only one set of five letters below can be arranged to spell out a five-letter English word. Find the word.

    BLEIT
    TONTE
    TIUNP
    GNEUR
    HEMUT

7.

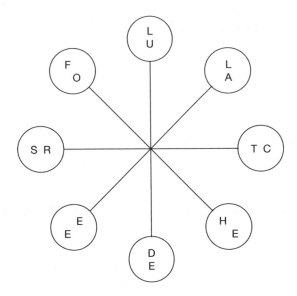

Find two eight-letter words that have opposite meanings by reading clockwise and, for each word, taking one letter at a time from each circle. Both words start at a different circle, but all letters in each word are in the correct order. Use each letter once each only.

8.   What is the meaning of assiduous?

a. living a strict life
b. forceful
c. persevering
d. ingenious
e. harsh or acidic

9. Find a familiar phrase reading clockwise. You have to find the starting point and insert the missing letters. Only alternate letters are shown.

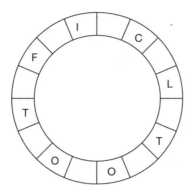

10. Work from letter to adjacent letter horizontally and verti-cally, but not diagonally, to spell out a 12-letter word. Use each letter once each only. You have to find the starting point, and provide the missing letters.

Numerical ability test

Calculators may be used in this test, if preferred.

1. Michael has £72 to spend. He spends 2/3 on computer software, then 0.375 of what he has left on lunch and finally £6 on a taxi home. What is his financial situation at the end of the day?

2. A merchant had six barrels of different sizes. They contained 15, 16, 18, 19, 20 and 31 litres respectively. Five of the barrels are full of wine and only one is full of water.

    The first customer bought two barrels of wine and the second customer bought twice as much wine as the first. The merchant returned home with the barrel of water. How much did it contain?

3. How many minutes is it before 12 noon, if 44 minutes ago it was three times as many minutes past 9 am?

4. Three brothers joined the army on the same day.

    Alf comes home once every five days, Sid comes home once every four days and Jim comes home once every 11 days. How often will all three meet up together?

5. What number should replace the question mark?

6. Three friends were playing poker.

Each player had a certain amount of money, in addition to which there was a pool of money in the centre of the table.

Alan said: *If I win this pool I will have twice as much money as both of you put together.*

Bernice said: *If I win this pool I will have three times as much money as both of you put together.*

Carol said: *If I win this pool I will have five times as much money as both of you put together.*

How much money was in the pool and how much money had each player?

7. What number continues the sequence?

   1   5   19   77   307   ?

8. A snail is climbing out of a well that is 10 feet deep. Every hour the snail climbs up 3 feet and slides back down 2 feet. How many hours will it take for the snail to escape from the well?

9. What number continues the sequence?

368, 406, 452, 494, 538, ?

10. Harry has a third as many again as Larry, who has a third as many again as Barry. Altogether they have 222.

How many has each?

Answers to IQ test one

Spatial ability test

1. D: the single larger circles are getting smaller. The smaller circles in between are increasing in number by one each time and getting larger from the bottom.

2. D: only lines that appear in the same position just twice in the first three squares are transferred to the final square. Only circles that appear in the same position just once are transferred.

3. F: A is the same as D, C is the same as G and B is the same as E.

4. E: looking both across and down only when the same figure appears in the same position in the first two squares is it transferred to the third square; however, circles then become rectangles and vice versa.

5. A: the number of sides on the outside figure decreases by one, but the number of sides on the inside figure increases by one.

6. E

7. B: The sequence of symbols runs:
    black dot/miss two squares/black dot; line at the top/miss three squares/line at the top; miss one square/diagonal line/miss one square; miss one square/vertical line/miss one square; miss two squares/white circle/miss two squares.

8. B: a quarter is added to the largest and smallest arcs moving clockwise. A quarter is added to the middle arc moving anti-clockwise.

9. D: the circle moves one corner anticlockwise at each stage, and the diagonal line moves two pairs of corners clockwise at each stage.

10. A: each horizontal and vertical line of shields contains three black stars and four white stars.

Logic test

1. develop: each word starts with the last and first letters, in that order, of the previous word.

2. 4: each number represents the number of digits that are adjacent to it either horizontally, vertically or diagonally.

3. K: the sequence runs:

    ABCdEfGhiJklMnopQrstUvwxyZabcdEfghijK

4. 76452: reverse and deduct one from the same number each time, that is, the number next to the 2.

5.

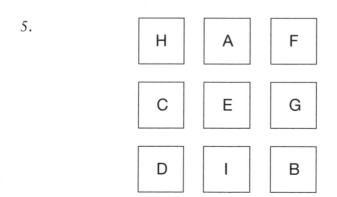

Replace each letter with its corresponding number in the alphabet to form a magic square in which each horizontal, vertical and corner to corner line totals 15.

6.   Colin is the strongest, followed by Carol, then Jill then Peter.

7.   2: all the others are a mirror image of their neighbour looking across and down.

8.   5: looking across and down, in each line the sum of alternate numbers total the same, for example, in the first line across, 3 + 8 + 9 = 13 + 7 (20).

9.   TSYX: reverse the first two and last two letters in each group. The sequence then progresses two consecutive letters, miss four, then two consecutive, for example, EDKJ becomes DE****JK.

10. 1836427: each number starts with the last five digits of the previous number, followed by the first two digits reversed.

Verbal ability test

1.   take good care of

2.   plausible, unlikely

3.   lava

4.   calm, agitated

5.   apologetic

6.   TUINP = input

7.   desolate, cheerful

8.   c. persevering

9. out of circulation

10. inexperience

Numerical ability test

1. £9 left: £72 less 2/3 = £24. 0.375 × £24 = £9, that is, £15 left less £6 = £9

2. 20 litres

first customer	second customer
15	16
18	19
33	31
	66

3. 34 minutes: 12 noon – 34 minutes = 11.26 am
    9 am + (34 × 3) = 102 minutes = 10.42 am
    11.26 – 10.42 = 44 minutes

4. Once every 220 days (5 × 4 × 11).

5. 2: 6 × 4 = 24/12 = 2. Similarly 3 × 20 = 60/12 = 5.

6. Pool = £15
    Alan = £1
    Bernice = £3
    Carol = £5

7. 1229: the sequence runs × 4 + 1 and × 4 – 1 alternately.

8. Eight hours: after one hour it climbs 1 foot. After seven hours it has climbed 7 feet. In the eighth hour it climbs the remaining 3 feet and is at the top, so does not slide back.

9. 596: add the number formed by the first and last digits each time, so 538 + 58 = 596.

10. Barry = 54, Larry = 72, Harry = 96

IQ test two

Introduction

IQ test two consists of a battery of 20 questions in a variety of different disciplines: spatial ability, logical thought processes, verbal ability and numerical ability. A time limit of 60 minutes is allowed for completing the 20 questions. You should keep strictly within your time limit, otherwise your score will be invalidated. Calculators may be used where preferred.

Performance rating
19–20 exceptional
16–18 excellent
13–15 very good
10–12 good
7–9   average

1.   Which is the odd one out?

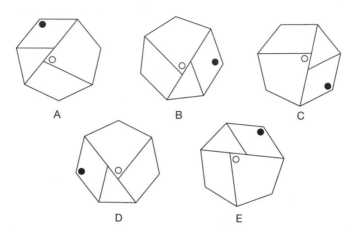

2.   Which word in brackets is most opposite to the word in capitals?

IRRATIONAL (concerned, circumspect, regular, purposed, indelible)

3.   What are the next two numbers in the sequence below?

1.5, 12.5, 3.25, 10.75, 5, 9, 6.75, 7.25

4.   Which two words are most opposite in meaning?

large, hopeful, wizened, fatuous, turgid, healthy

5.   Insert the numbers 1–6 in the circles so that for any particular circle the sum of the numbers in the circles connected directly to it equals the value corresponding to the number in that circle as given in the list.

Example:

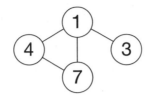

1 = 14 (4 + 7 + 3)
4 = 8 (7 + 1)
7 = 5 (4 + 1)
3 = 1

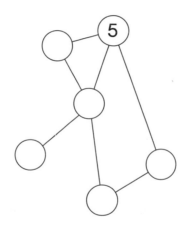

1 = 9
2 = 6
3 = 11
4 = 7
5 = 10
6 = 14

6.

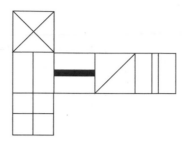

When the above is folded to form a cube, which one of the following can be produced?

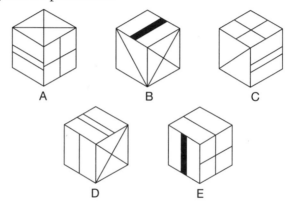

7.   Which two words are closest in meaning?

quiddity, espousal, effluence, tension, support, literate

8.   What numbers should replace the question marks?

7	6	2	5	1
8	9	6	3	2
1	7	8	6	1
2	4	7	3	1
9	1	6	6	1
2	5	3	?	?

9.

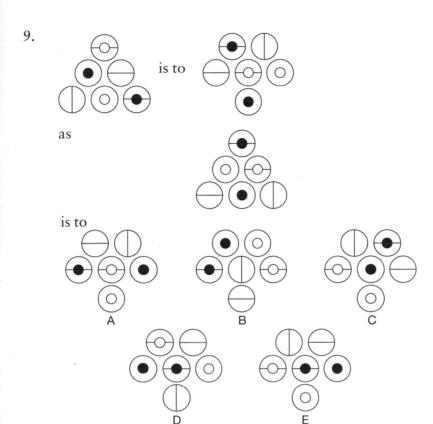

10. DISCLAIM is to repudiate as abdure is to: waive, forsake, forgo, forfeit, renounce

11. What numbers should replace the question marks?

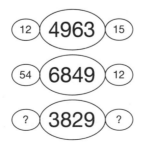

12.

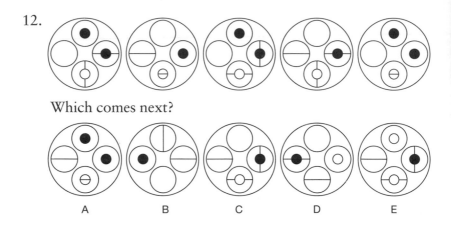

Which comes next?

A	B	C	D	E

13. Which of the following is *not* an anagram of a country?

hug yarn
teen pun
ink pasta
big mule
into sea

14. A batsman is out for 68 runs, which raises his batting average for the season from 32 to 36. How many runs would he have had to have scored to raise his average for the season to 39?

15. Find the starting point and follow the instructions to arrive at the treasure, marked **T**. Visit *every* square once each only.

1E 2S	2S 1E	1S 2W
T	1S 1W	2W 1N
1N 2E	2N 1E	1N 1W

1E
2S   means one square east, then two squares south

16.

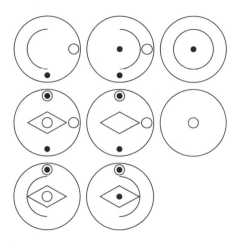

Which is the missing circle?

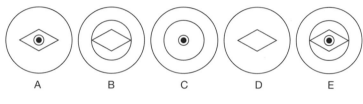

A   B   C   D   E

17. A   B   C   D   E   F   G   H

What letter is two to the left of the letter that comes immediately to the right of the letter that comes four to the left of the letter that comes two to the right of the letter E?

18. Change one letter only from each of the words below to produce a familiar phrase.

POUT ON CALF

19. Each of the nine squares marked 1A to 3C incorporates all the lines and symbols that are shown in the squares of the same letter and number immediately above and to the left. For example, 2B should incorporate all the lines and symbols contained in 2 and B.

However, one of the squares is incorrect. Can you find it?

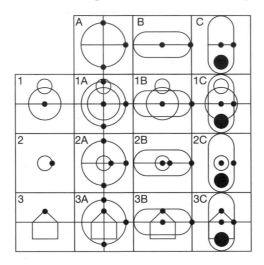

20.

Barry lives 4 miles west of Alice
Carol lives 3 miles south of Barry
David lives 2 miles west of Carol
Elizabeth lives 1 mile north of David
Fiona lives 3 miles east of Elizabeth
Gareth lives 4 miles north of Fiona
Harry lives 1 mile west of Gareth.

How far, and in what direction, does Harry live from Barry?

Answers to IQ test two

1. B: the rest are the same figure rotated.

2. circumspect

3. 8.5 and 5.5: there are two sequences beginning with 1.5 and 12.5. The first increases by 1.75 and the second reduces by 1.75.

4. wizened, turgid

5.

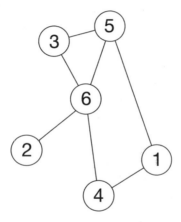

6. B

7. espousal, support

8. 0 1

    In each line add the first three numbers, then reverse the answer to obtain the last two numbers. So: 2 + 5 + 3 = 10, which reversed = 01.

9. E: the symbols change positions exactly as in the first analogy, for example, the symbol bottom left moves to top right.

10. forsake

11. $3 \times 9 = 27$ and $8 + 2 = 10$

12. C: looking across, the top circle alternates dot/empty, the left circle alternates empty/horizontal line, the right circle alternates black dot with horizontal line/black dot/black dot with vertical line, and the bottom circle alternates white dot with vertical line/white dot with internal horizontal line/white dot with horizontal line.

13. teen pun = Neptune. The countries are Hungary = hug yarn, Pakistan = ink pasta, Belgium = big mule and Estonia = into sea

14. 95

    8 innings average 32 = 256
    9 innings average 36 = 324
    9 innings average 39 = 351

    256 + 68 = 324; 256 + 95 = 351

15.

6	1	8
T	3	5
4	7	2

16. C: looking both across and down, only symbols that appear once only in the same position in the first two circles are carried forward to the third circle.

17. B

18. port of call

19. 2C

20. 2 miles north